The
All-Lover All-Star Team
and 50 Other Improbable
Baseball Lineups

The
All-Lover All-Star Team
and 50 Other Improbable
Baseball Lineups

Al Davis and Elliot Horne

William Morrow and Company, Inc.
New York

Recognizing the importance of preserving what has been written, it is the policy of William Morrow and Company, Inc., and its imprints and affiliates to have the books it publishes printed on acid-free paper, and we exert our best efforts to that end.

Library of Congress Cataloging-in-Publication Data

Davis, Al.
The all-lover all-star team
/ Al Davis and Elliot Horne.
p.   cm.
ISBN 0-688-09621-2
1. Baseball—United States—Miscellanea.   2. Baseball—United States—Humor.   I. Horne, Elliot.   II. Title.
GV867.3.D39   1990
796.357′0973—dc20   89-29541
                                                                                            CIP

Printed in the United States of America

First Edition

1 2 3 4 5 6 7 8 9 10

BOOK DESIGN BY JAYE ZIMET

To Elliot, my beloved coauthor and partner, who made me read *Shoeless Joe* long before it became *Field of Dreams,* and who stole home much too soon

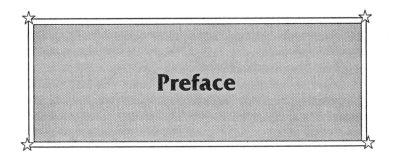

Preface

This all started as a game on a slow day at the office.

The idea for this collection of unusual all-star teams came up as a substitute for my continual passionate arguments about sports with my late partner and coauthor, Elliot Horne—arguments the violence of which was beginning to frighten people in neighboring offices.

To be perfectly honest, the arguments didn't really stop, but at least now they were to a constructive purpose.

They were also a lot of fun.

I can't explain why baseball, of all sports, lavishes so many and varied pleasures on American fans. We enjoy not only playing it and watching it and arguing about it and throwing punches over it (check out the upper stands at Shea Stadium on a crowded, hot August night), we also can't get enough of it off the field. The endless diet of card shows, rotisserie leagues, radio call-in shows, can't seem to assuage our appetite for the stately game. (Stately in concept certainly, if not in crotch-scratching, chaw-spitting actuality.)

Then there are the books. Baseball demands to be written about. No other sport I can think of has so much the novelistic architecture that is in every single ball game ever played. The combination of single combat—pitcher versus batter—and team conflict, makes for as ravishing an experience as reading *The Iliad* or a good western.

One of the best things about a project like this is that you find yourself building up a baseball library, ostensibly for research purposes (as you insist to your wife), until you realize that the project is finished but you are still buying baseball books.

The pleasures of baseball.

My first baseball experience was not that pleasurable. My father took me, aged three and a half, to the 1926 World Series (Cards and Yanks), the famous game in which the elderly Grover Cleveland Alexander struck out the rookie phenom Tony Lazzeri in the clutch. My vivid memory is of trying to see the distant green field through a forest of legs—the bleacher fans in front of us were standing up a lot—pestering my father for some candy and having to go to the bathroom in perfect timing for my father to miss a Ruthian homer.

Paraphrasing Shaw, baseball is too precious to be wasted on infants. Also, that may have had something to do with my becoming, a few years later, a fanatical Giant fan.*

In this humble addition to the marvelous existing library of baseball books, we have tried hard to be original. I don't think anybody else has come up with any of the great majority of our teams. The one exception I can think of is the Jewish All-Star Team, which for some reason nobody seems able to resist, including us. I believe our commentary does make even our Jewish All-Star Team different.

Actually, we rejected the basic concept of obvious ethnic all-star teams for that very reason—they are too obvious. How difficult could it be to assemble a Black All-Star Team for example? Or Italian, Polish, Irish, or WASP all-star teams?

Our few ethnic teams were chosen for their unique interest. (See Dominican Republic All-Star Team or Native-American All-Star Team.)

But let's not, please, get too serious. As one typical argumentative, dogmatic, prejudiced, fanatical baseball addict to another, let's fight.

—AL DAVIS

*The New York *baseball* Giants, to be precise

Acknowledgments

The limerick about Goose Gossage was written by Elliot Horne.

All notes were written by Al Davis.

Statistics are complete through the 1989 season.

It would be impossible to recall the names of all the hundreds of writers whose books, magazine and newspaper articles, and radio and TV interviews we have absorbed over the years. Here are a few whose work we have especially enjoyed, in no particular order: Joe Reichler, Lawrence Ritter, Donald Honig, Dick Bartell, Robert Creamer, Bill James, Dan Parker, Willard Mullin, Jimmy Cannon, Ring Lardner, Bill Corum, Frank Graham, Red Barber, Russ Hodges, Roger Kahn, Red Smith, Ron Luciano, Grantland Rice, Arch McDonald, Tom Boswell, Art Hill, Art Hano, Jerome Charyn, Peter Gammons, David Halberstam, Roger Angell, et al.

All-Star Teams

12

The
All-Lover All-Star Team
and 50 Other Improbable
Baseball Lineups

1

The
Ducky, Lucky, Bucky, Cookie, Tookie, Mookie, Mickey, Mackey, Jackie All-Star Team

First Base	**"Ducky" Medwick**
Second Base	**"Lucky" Lohrke**
Shortstop	**"Bucky" Dent**
Third Base	**"Cookie" Lavagetto**
Outfield	**"Tookie" Gilbert**
	"Mookie" Wilson
	"Mickey" Mantle
Catcher	**"Mackey" Sasser**
Pitcher	**"Jackie" Brown**

2

High Average (Season) All-Star Team

First Base	**George Sisler**	.420	1922
Second Base	**Napoleon Lajoie**	.422	1901
Shortstop	**Rogers Hornsby**	.424	1924 (1)
Third Base	**George Brett**	.390	1980
Outfield	**Ty Cobb**	.420	1911
	Joe Jackson	.408	1911
	Ted Williams	.406	1941
Catcher	**Jimmie Foxx**	.364	1932 (2)
Pitcher	**George Uhle**	.361	1923 (3)

High Average (Season)
All-Star Team
Notes

(1) While it is true that Hornsby was a second baseman for the preponderance of his career, he started as a shortstop, and played the equivalent of more than two seasons in that position. Interesting oddity: The two highest batting averages of the twentieth century were produced by second basemen, normally one of the lighter hitting positions.

(2) Admittedly, Foxx played only 109 of his 2,317 games at catcher, but he retained his pads and mitt throughout his career, and did some catching almost every season. Not satisfied? Okay, Bill Dickey batted .362 in 1936.

(3) While I have fudged by using former pitchers in this slot when batting prowess is needed, I have formulated rules of forgivable fudging. Under these rules, I permit myself two uses of Babe Ruth as a pitcher (see HOME RUN All-Star Teams). Actually, Sisler also started in the majors as a pitcher, so I could, in moderate conscience, have switched his .420 BA to this team's pitching slot. This would have enabled me to fill first base with one of my personal favorites, Bill Terry and his .401. But I am a man of honor, and can be counted on to hold my finagling down to a minimum.

High Average (Career) All-Star Team*

First Base	**Bill Terry**	**.341**
Second Base	**Rogers Hornsby**	**.358**
Shortstop	**Honus Wagner**	**.329**
Third Base	**Wade Boggs**	**.356**
Outfield	**Ty Cobb**	**.367**
	Joe Jackson	**.356**
	"Wee Willie" Keeler	**.345**
	Ed Delahanty	**.345**
Catcher	**Jimmie Foxx**	**.325**
Pitcher	**George Uhle**	**.288**

High Average (Career)
All-Star Team
Notes

*My policy for statistics-determined teams has been to stay with modern era players. Numbers put up prior to the twentieth century are suspect, because of the inconsistent standards and conditions then prevailing. Unquestionably, many nineteenth-century players would have been stars in any era, as a glance at the records of some who excelled across the 1890s and early 1900s would seem to attest. Thus, "Wee Willie" Keeler and Ed Delahanty, who fall into that crossover category, make the team, ahead of moderns Ted Williams and Tris Speaker, whose mutual .344 lifetime BAs fall a single point behind those of the earlier superstars. (I still haven't figured out how Delahanty managed to hit four homers in one game in that lead-ball epoch. He had to have been a monster.) On the other hand, hulking first baseman Dan Brouthers, a lifetime .343 hitter, is disqualified by virtue of having been born ten years too soon, as is .341 batter "Cap" Anson, probably the late nineteenth century's greatest star and manager. It was a pleasure banning Anson from this team, in the knowledge that he had been the individual primarily responsible for banning Blacks from baseball for half a century.

Incidentally, it is by just a single point that Terry beats out the greatest-hitting first baseman of all time, Lou Gehrig, a .340 man.

Again I shift Foxx to catcher, not because I need a

catcher for this team—in this instance, Mickey Cochrane's .320 lifetime number would qualify nicely—but because it would be an injustice to keep him off the team. In my opinion he must be ranked among the ten greatest hitters in the history of the game.

The pitching situation for this team is interesting. Only eight points separate the three most talented hitting pitchers (not counting "the Bambino," of course; if he's in the running, it's no contest). Red Lucas batted .281 and Wes Ferrell hit .280, all three (including Uhle) over long careers as highly successful pitchers. Just think, had there been a designated hitter rule going during their careers, I could have saved six and a half lines of type. Of course, I could always have put in a designated typist.

4

Flake
All-Star Team

First Base	**Joe Pepitone (1)**
Second Base	**Rod Kanehl (2)**
Shortstop	**Phil Linz (3)**
Third Base	**Rocky Bridges (4)**
Outfield	**Jimmy Piersall (5)**
	Dick Allen (6)
	Frenchy Bordagaray (7)
	Babe Herman (8)
	John Lowenstein (9)
Catcher	**Bob Uecker (10)**
Pitcher	**Billy Loes (11)**

Flake
All-Star Team
Notes

(1) We have here, with Pepitone, several major league firsts—first hot comb in a clubhouse locker, first toupee worn by an active player, first New York–born player to prove that native New Yorkers can be as dumb as anybody. (See also: DRUG ABUSER All-Star Team, etc.)

(2) Kanehl is most famous for having once taken literally Mets manager Casey Stengel's throwaway line that, as a reward for a good pinch-running stint, he could stay in the game (this remark, it must be said in defense of the Ol' Perfessor, was during the team's legendary "What difference does it make?" era). "Where?" asked Kanehl. "Anywhere you want," said Casey and shrugged, anxious to get back to his doze. Kanehl proceeded to bench the third baseman and shift the other regulars around to make an opening for himself in the infield. He is also fondly remembered for his willingness to "take one on the ass for the team," an approach that earned him the lead in getting hit by pitches for three straight years. Interestingly, Ron Hunt, who beat him out for the second base position on the Mets, and went on to become the fledgling team's first legitimate all-star, also succeeded Kanehl as a virtuoso in getting plunked by the pitcher—and possibly even as an all-star flake. It is sad that because of limited space all the Mets flakes cannot make the FLAKE All-Star Team, since

they could fill out such a team by themselves. I doubt whether even the notorious Brooklyn Dodger "Daffiness Boys" of the thirties could outflake the likes of Marv Throneberry, Choo Choo Coleman, Cleon Jones, Ron Swoboda, Jay Hook, Tug McGraw, Dave Kingman, Frank Thomas, Tim Foli—not to mention such more recent candidates as Len Dykstra, Darryl Strawberry, Sid Fernandez, Randy Meyers, et al.

(3) Linz postponed his career as a nightspot owner by playing for the Yankees and Mets for several years as a utility infielder. His most famous incident: having a harmonica yanked out of his mouth by Yankees manager Yogi Berra on the team bus after a tough loss. His most deathless line: his ultimatum to the Yankees, at a press conference he called to "clarify my status." "Play me," he demanded angrily, "or keep me!"

(4) Interchangeable with Phil Linz. I don't know what it is about utility infielders, but they do seem to make the best flakes.

(5) Piersall is certainly the only ballplayer ever to testify to his own psychological diagnosis through a major motion picture that documents his clinical problems (*Fear Strikes Out*: see BROADWAY/HOLLYWOOD All-Star Team). He still managed seventeen productive years in the big leagues, marred only by the occasional tantrum or fistfight. Maybe not so occasional, on second thought, but what the hell. Any man who could field like he did and run the bases backward when he hit his hundredth home run deserves some consideration.

(6) Dick Allen is a leading candidate for most talented underachiever ever to dominate an era. His casual approach to his profession—which he indicated came second in his priorities to his horse-breeding avocation—could scarcely diminish his enormous impact. He led his league once each in RBI and runs, twice in home runs, and three times in slugging average—without half trying. What would he have

accomplished had his heart really been in it? A peek into the workings of the Allen mind was provided by such acts as his sudden announcement to the media that after years of stardom under the name of Richie, he must henceforth be called Dick. Why? Why not? Former teammate Bob Uecker insists Allen used to alert his teammates that he would take two strikes at bat "to see what I can do with one shot."

(7) Frenchy, who vied with Babe Herman for the title of goofiest Brooklyn Dodger during the thirties when that signified the ultimate in on-field bizarrerie, provided then-manager Casey Stengel with some of his more stressful experiences as well as some of his greatest anecdotes. Every collector of baseball lore is familiar with the most famous Bordagaray howler. He was tagged out off second base, after having been specifically lectured by Stengel on the urgency of staying on the base, and he excused himself to Stengel by proudly reporting, "Casey, I bet I wasn't more than half an inch off the base." With the passage of the years, Stengel improved on the story (as every great raconteur will) with an alternative version in which Frenchy swore, "Casey, I never moved off the base. I was tapping my foot on the base the whole time." "So how come," inquired Stengel, "the ump called you out?" "He must have tagged me between taps," Frenchy allegedly explained. Then there was the time Bordagaray's cap came off as he was pursuing a deep drive to the outer reaches of Ebbets Field. Unlike the frequent case with "Say Hey Kid" Mays, Frenchy did not outrun the ball and make a memorable catch. Possibly because he felt called upon to go back and pick up his hat and reset it on his head before resuming pursuit of the ball. The one I like best is when, during a pregame warm-up, Bordagaray hit Stengel in the head with an errant throw. Stengel was taken off the field for medical treatment, and the game proceeded with one of the coaches managing. In a rare occurrence for those days, the Dodgers happened to win the game. The next day, when the still groggy Stengel arrived at the ballpark, Bordagaray was waiting for him. "Casey, that turned out to be lucky for the

team. Why don't we do it again, and maybe we'll get lucky again and win another one?"

(8) Herman is best remembered for the most notorious bonehead play in baseball history, the one where he hit a double into a double play. According to Dick Bartell, Herman was the least culpable of the three base runners involved, but he was the notoriously eccentric "Babe" and the team was the equally notoriously nutty Dodgers, so the rap has stayed with him through the years. Personally, I much prefer his play when, with three men on in the bottom of the ninth inning, and the outfield drawn in for a throw to the plate on a sharp base hit, fortune smiled and the batter lined a sharp base hit—just what the doctor ordered—straight at Herman. As the opposing team groaned in anticipation that Herman, who had one of the stronger arms in the league, would easily force the lead runner at the plate, the Babe deftly fielded the ball, shoved it into his back pocket, and raced off the field to the clubhouse. Probably had a heavy date waiting—assuming he survived his prior date with apoplectic manager Chuck Dressen.

(9) "Steiner" Lowenstein once feigned unconsciousness after being hit by a thrown ball. Not until he was being carted off the hushed field on a stretcher did he show a sign of life, by leaping out of the stretcher and screaming at the top of his lungs, to the huge delight of his many fans, who typically lavished more affection on their team's brain-damaged, lesser-talented part-timers than on the superstars. Lowenstein also had his own switch on Phil Linz's "Play me or keep me!" ultimatum to the Yankees. Lowenstein urged the Orioles management to "Play me or pay me!," claiming that utility players deserved more money than regulars, on the grounds that sitting on the bench entailed substantial health risks because of the sudden physical activity required by being unexpectedly called into a game.

(10) Bob Uecker. Need I say more?

(11) Author of possibly the greatest excuse ever offered for misplaying a ground ball in a World Series: "I lost it in the sun." He also shared one of the more profound observations about the Mets in their early futile period: "The Mets is a very good thing. They give everybody a job. Just like the WPA." Despite brilliant pitching skills, playing on a Brooklyn team that won three pennants, he never won more than fourteen games in a season—intentionally, it is almost unanimously believed. Loes implied he could have collected many more victories. "But if you win twenty games, they expect you to do it every year."

We can't take our leave of this delightful gang without mentioning one of the great characters of baseball, left-hander Vernon "Lefty" Gomez. He brings back memories of our youth, when, as a Hall of Fame–bound star of the Joe McCarthy Yankees, he regularly beat my Giants in the World Series. For some reason, he is known these days by his second nickname, "Lefty." Nobody seems to remember that when he was active his nickname was "Goofy." And while he could be charged with doing such flaky things as pausing in the middle of his windup to follow the flight of a plane overhead, in my opinion he was the wittiest man who ever donned cleats. When Jimmie Foxx hit an enormous home run off him into the third deck of Yankee Stadium, Gomez cracked, "If I was on that sonofabitch I'd be back in California by now." He had another line about Foxx, whose imposing physique must have figured in the nightmares of many a pitcher. When asked why he'd gotten rid of the glasses he'd been using toward the end of his career, the Goofy One snapped, "They gave me too good a look at Foxx's arms."

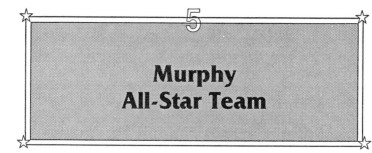

5

Murphy
All-Star Team

First Base	**"Morg" Murphy**
Second Base	**"Soldier Boy" Murphy**
Shortstop	**"Dummy" Murphy**
Third Base	**"Dirty Dave" Murphy**
Outfield	**"Gentle Willie" Murphy**
	"Honest Eddie" Murphy
	"Tot Midget" Murphy
Catcher	**"Stone Face" Murphy**
Pitcher	**"Razzle Dazzle" Murphy**

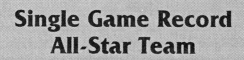

Single Game Record
All-Star Team

First Base	**Jim Bottomley**	**16 runs batted in**
Second Base	**Rennie Stennett**	**7 base hits**
Shortstop	**Cesar Gutierrez**	**7 base hits**
Third Base	**Frank Robinson**	**Back-to-back grand slams in successive innings**
Outfield	**Joe Adcock**	**18 total bases**
	Gene Stephens	**3 hits in one inning**
	Josh Devore	**4 stolen bases in one inning**
Catcher	**Jimmie Foxx**	**6 bases on balls**
Pitcher	**Harvey Haddix**	**12 perfect innings**

Basketball Player All-Star Team

First Base	**Chuck Connors**	**(Seton Hall) (1)**
Second Base	**Jackie Robinson**	**(UCLA) (2)**
Shortstop	**Dick Groat**	**(Duke) (3)**
Third Base	**Danny Ainge**	**(Brigham Young) (4)**
Outfield	**Frank Howard**	**(Ohio State) (5)**
	Tony Gwynn	**(San Diego State) (6)**
	Dave Winfield	**(Minnesota) (7)**
Catcher	**Lou Boudreau**	**(Illinois) (8)**
Pitcher	**Gene Conley**	**(Washington State) (9)**

Basketball Player
All-Star Team
Notes

(1) Connors, the doughty "Rifleman" of TV fame, was one of the few men to play in both the NBA and the major baseball leagues. (Others include Dick Groat, Danny Ainge, Gene Conley, and Dave DeBusschere.) He also holds the distinction of being probably the least talented baseball player on any of my all-star teams. But he did have one at bat for the Brooklyn Dodgers in 1949, and played in sixty-six games with the Cubs during the '51 season. It would probably be an injustice to attribute the Cubs' last-place finish that year entirely to Connors's presence on the roster. That team had ample lack of talent to distribute the blame equitably.

(2) Robinson was the first and only athlete in UCLA's history to win letters in four varsity sports—baseball, football, basketball, and track—all, remarkably, accomplished in his freshman and sophomore years. (After that he left for the army in World War II, attaining the rank of captain.) In basketball, Robinson led the PAC 10's Southern Division in scoring in 1939 and 1940. It probably didn't hurt his hoops game that he was a good enough jumper to win the 1940 NCAA long-jump championship. (See FOOTBALL PLAYER All-Star Team for more of Robinson's nonbaseball athletic exploits.)

(3) In my opinion the best basketball player on the team, Groat was a three-time All-American at Duke, and starred for the NBA's Fort Wayne Pistons (later to become the Detroit Pistons) before breaking in with the Pirates. He led the league in batting (.325 in 1960, which happens to be the year Mazeroski homered the Yankees out of the World Series in that memorable ninth inning). He also played a lot of shortstop, leading the league once in assists, four times each in put-outs and total chances per game, and five times in double plays. The fact that he also led the league six times in errors should not diminish his achievement—the more chances, the more errors, right?

(4) The fortuitous circumstance that this team has to have a third baseman permits Ainge to make the roster. He did play 80 games at the position for Toronto—more than a third of his 211-game major league career. The best that can be said of Ainge, a lifetime .220 hitter, is that as a baseball player he was a pretty good basketball player. Only the presence of Chuck Connors at first base saves Ainge from being the least gifted baseballer on the team.

(5) Howard was a bigger basketball than baseball star at Ohio State. He was team captain; led the squad in scoring, field goal percentage, and rebounds; and made All Big 10 in 1958. Incidentally, he is the twenty-second leading scorer in OSU history (which includes such names as John Havlicek and Jerry Lucas).

(6) Gwynn actually attended college on a basketball scholarship, led the Western Conference in assists for two years, and badly outplayed Danny Ainge in a game against Brigham Young. He was drafted in the tenth round by the then San Diego Clippers, but opted to heed the call of the Padres, who had drafted him third. It would be interesting to know who the two players were that San Diego drafted ahead of the soon-to-be most prolific batter in the National League.

(7) Winfield's extraordinary athletic skills, so apparent in his effortless virtuosity for the Yankees, make it less than sur-

prising to read this quote by Bill Musselman, Winfield's basketball coach at the University of Minnesota, who claims big Dave was the best player he ever coached. "I don't think it's close. . . . He's one of the best rebounders I've ever coached and that includes Jim Brewer, Bill Laimbeer, and Mark Olberding." Are you reading, Herr Steinbrenner?

(8) Although he is a Hall of Fame shortstop, I take poetic license here in arbitrarily positioning Boudreau at catcher, on the flimsy if necessary ground that he donned the pads three times in his Frank Merriwellian career—once each in three separate seasons. Actually, he came up to Cleveland as a third baseman, and but for Ken Keltner, who had arrived a year previously and staked an unshakable claim on Cleveland's hot corner, Boudreau's career might well have been at that position. Keltner and Boudreau, not a bad duo to anchor the left side of anybody's infield. As for baskets, the sweet-swinging shortstop—I mean catcher—starred in roundball at Illinois, where he was noted for his good hands and spectacular dribbling skills.

(9) Conley posted a 91 and 96 record in eleven years in the Bigs, playing for the Braves, Phillies, and Red Sox. Part of that time he also played center for the Celtics. Not in Dave DeBusschere's league as a basketball player, nor as good as Groat in baseball, Conley, all things considered, was a better than average performer in both sports. DeBusschere's big league pitching career never got off the ground. He put in two years with the White Sox, appearing in 36 games and compiling a record of three wins and four losses, in a career total of 102 and one third innings.

Sissy All-Star Team

First Base	**Kitty Bransfield**
Second Base	**Nellie Fox**
Shortstop	**Sadie Hauck**
Third base	**Lena Blackburne**
Outfield	**Judy Johnson**
	Estel Crabtree
	Sis Hopkins
Catcher	**Peaches Graham**
Pitcher	**Molly Craft**

Gold Glove
All-Star Team*

First Base	**Keith Hernandez**	**11-time winner**
Second Base	**Bill Mazeroski**	**8-time winner**
	Frank White	**8-time winner**
Shortstop	**Luis Aparicio**	**9-time winner**
	Ozzie Smith	**9-time winner**
Third Base	**Brooks Robinson**	**16-time winner**
Outfield	**Willie Mays**	**12-time winner**
	Roberto Clemente	**12-time winner**
	Al Kaline	**10-time winner**
Catcher	**Johnny Bench**	**10-time winner**
Pitcher	**Jim Kaat**	**16-time winner**

Gold Glove
All-Star Team
Notes

*Since this award dates back only to 1957, allowance must be made for three contingencies: (1) those whose careers were several seasons along when the Gold Glove was instituted in 1957—Mays, Aparicio, Kaline, Malzone, Mazeroski, Hodges, Vic Power, and a few others who might have been expected to win more Gold Gloves; (2) those whose careers ended prematurely—Clemente, Flood, Campanella; and of course (3) those legendary fielding virtuosi who played before there was such a thing as a Gold Glove Award—the Tris Speakers, Joe DiMaggios, Hal Chases, Honus Wagners. From personal observation, only Bill Terry and Babe Dahlgren ranked with Hernandez as fielders. While I recall them as being more graceful and effortless in their play, I don't recall ever seeing any first baseman make some of the plays Hernandez pulls off routinely. Joe Gordon and Charlie Gehringer are the best I ever saw around the keystone sack. Gordon was explosively quick and lived up to his nickname, "Flash." Gehringer was as pretty and economical, and made the impossible plays look as easy as Mikhail Baryshnikov executing multiple entrechats. Leo Durocher, despite his designation as "the Hitless Wonder," earned his keep on famous teams like the '27 Yanks and as Frank Frisch's mid-infield partner on "the Gashouse Gang" Cardinals of the thirties, by being the outstanding shortstop of that era. Phil Rizzuto, who came up as Durocher (by now Brooklyn's manager) was phasing himself out as a player, shared the distinction with Marty Marion as being the best of their time. Hey, you Old-Timers Committee, please induct "the Scooter" into his deserved niche in the Hall of Fame while he's alive. Pee Wee Reese, his opposite number, is lonesome without him up there in Cooperstown. Another personal observation: Like Hernandez at first base, Ozzie Smith makes plays I have never seen any other shortstop make. So did Brooks Robinson, who took the playing of third base to a new dimension. My personal all-time outfield would have to be even deeper than the old Polo Grounds to accommodate all the guys I want playing for my team out there. Terry Moore, Joe D., Willie Mays, Roberto Clemente, Curt Flood, Duke Snider, Al Kaline, Fred Lynn, Roger Maris, Paul Blair, Yaz—not too shabby a list, I submit. Of today's crop, here is a group I would match against almost any of my historic favorites: Andre Dawson, RF; Andy Van Slyke, CF; and Kevin McReynolds, LF. Of the old-time catchers, in my recollection, Al Lopez was the smoothest receiver and shrewdest strategist, Bill Dickey and Mickey Cochrane the most physically talented (Bench reminds me of Dickey), and Roy Campanella an amalgam of all these virtues. Fred Fitzsimmons and Bobby Shantz were the class fielding pitchers. In Fitzsimmons's case, this was rather remarkable since he was heavy to the point of being nicknamed "Fat Freddie." Added to which he had a peculiar delivery, winding up with his back to the batter (somewhat similar to "The Mad Hungarian," Al Hrabosky, the intimidating reliever of a few years back), then whirling around like a top to deliver his tough knuckler. Perhaps Fitz was like those agile, graceful dancers—the Jackie Gleasons and Fat Jack Leonards of the world. Shantz, also seemingly at a physical disadvantage at just five feet six inches, played his position like an only slightly less acrobatic Ozzie Smith.

10

Lead Glove
All-Star Team

First Base	**Dick Stuart (1)**
Second Base	**Chuck Hiller (2)**
	Steve Sax (3)
Shortstop	**Vern Stephens (4)**
Third Base	**Harmon Killebrew (5)**
Outfield	**Smead Jolley (6)**
	Dusty Rhodes (7)
	Darryl Strawberry (8)
Catcher	**Choo Choo Coleman (9)**
Pitcher	**Dennis Eckersley (10)**

Lead Glove
All-Star Team
Notes

(1) First base is the position with more candidates for lead-glove designation than any other for an obvious reason: It is the position of last resort for outfielders who can no longer run, infielders who can no longer cover ground, catchers who can no longer throw. Stuart, a leading candidate for the FLAKE All-Star Team as well, receives the palm over such other world-class nonfielders as Marv Throneberry and Zeke Bonura (slowest man ever to play the game) because his nickname makes good copy. Stuart's *nom de baseball* was "Dr. Strangeglove"—but of course you knew that.

(2) Confirming Hiller's qualifications for this team, even the staid *Baseball Encyclopedia* cites his well-earned nickname as second baseman of the Giants and Mets of the 1960s: "Iron Hands."

(3) For a long stretch, the boxes behind first base at Dodger Stadium were a hazardous zone, under constant strafing by baseballs launched by the powerful gun of the otherwise talented Mister Sax. Remarkable how this scatter-arm can go on offense and thread a needle through any infield with a bat in his hand. Maybe the gifted bat-control specialist should take his favorite stick out to his fielding position and fungo the ball to first base.

(4) Only a strong sense of honor prevented me from awarding the palm to my sentimental favorite, Mike Phil-

lips. He came along at a time of transition for me—when I was finally, painfully, cutting the umbilical cord from the old New York Giants and taking the new New York Mets to my bosom—and he came from the what were now the San Francisco Giants to the Mets, for whom he spelled the superb Bud Harrelson in the fading years of both their careers. Was it the stark contrast to Harrelson's extraordinary shortstop play that forever stamped Phillips, in my mind, as a joke at the position? I don't think so. I sincerely believe he earned my opinion of his fielding (I acknowledge he did come up with some timely hits) by a clumsiness remarkable in so well-set-up an athlete. I would have to say, Phillips's bad fielding was a gift. However, his career was slight, undeserving of so weighty an honor as placement on the LEAD GLOVE All-Star Team. That position truly belongs to Vern Stephens, who had lead legs to go with the glove, and he was instrumental in the semisuccess of the near-great Red Sox team of the late forties and early fifties—the team that was always almost beating the Yankees for the American League pennant every year. Almost, but not quite, at least partly because the Red Sox had Stephens clodhopping at shortstop, while the Yankees had Cora Rizzuto's hubby effortlessly covering that area like a tent.

(5) The late, great sports columnist Red Smith claimed that Killebrew's teammates said of his play at third base: "He hasn't much range, but anything he can get to, he'll drop." Pedro Guerrero said all there was to say about his own play at third base when, as the story goes, Tommy Lasorda asked him during a Dodgers skull session what he would be thinking in a certain crucial game situation. "I'm thinking," Pedro allegedly admitted, "dear Lord, please don't let them hit the ball to me!" We cannot leave the position without doing justice to sometime Giants third sacker Enos Cabell, of whom his bemused manager, Frank Robinson, once said, "I've never seen anyone get hit by so many balls in the field without even touching them as Cabell."

(6) Jolley had only four years in the Bigs despite a fearsome bat. An authentic .300 hitter, he never solved the fielding side of the equation and it cost him a promising

career. Jolley's was the klutziness that legends are made of. The one I like involves his problems with the outfield at Fenway Park, which during his tenure still had an uphill grade toward the left-field wall. Red Fox outfielders had always been forced to adjust to the topography, and so deftly had Jolley's predecessor, Duffy Lewis, navigated the area, it got to be known as Duffy's Hill. As far as Jolley was concerned, it could have been called Smead's Precipice. He certainly didn't feel he deserved any blame for his hair-raising performances in left field. After all, as he explained, "they taught me how to run up the cliff, but they never taught me how to run down it." Makes sense to me.

(7) Watching Rhodes trying to play right field at the old Polo Grounds was like watching the Indy 500. Not because he was fast (he wasn't) but because you knew a spectacular accident might happen. Dusty murdered pitchers for two years as a key member of Leo Durocher's Giants (the team that swept Cleveland in the '54 Series), but he gave the impression, when time came to patrol his outfield post, that fielding was some heathen ritual that really wasn't any of his business. When Dusty's sweet home run stroke—so perfectly tailored to the Polo Grounds' infamous 259-foot right-field wall—deserted him (drowned in a sea of Jack Daniels) he was gone and with him, the sense of adventure his pursuit of a fly ball inspired.

(8) One of my saddest judgments, because of Darryl's essentially sweet disposition and his enormous potential in every phase of the game, not to mention the impressive offensive achievements that have made him the most feared hitter in the National League. Unfortunately, he is also one of the most feared fielders—by Mets pitchers. To date, he has not seemed committed to improving his dreadful play in the outfield, where he is too often guilty of holding the ball too long, a lackadaisical pursuit of balls hit in his direction, an embarrassing inability to adjust for the sun in fielding fly balls, hotdogging one-handed "sidesaddle" catches (and misses), and horrendous decisions on which base to throw to.

(9) Choo Choo was your ideal quintuple threat—couldn't hit, couldn't hit with power, couldn't run, couldn't throw, and couldn't field. His catching feats in the early glory years of Mets futility had Casey Stengel rethinking his famous truism about a catcher being necessary—because without one you would get a lot of passed balls. "On the other hand, with Coleman back there, it don't hardly make any difference."

(10) If you disagree, take it up with Elliot's friend Stu Fine, a fanatical Red Sox fan, whose opinions on baseball I respect profoundly. For him still to be holding a grudge from the time when Eckersley was with Boston, the transgressions must have been pretty flagrant.

11

Unpronounceable Name All-Star Team

First Base	**Kent Hrbek**
Second Base	**Rocky Krsnich**
Shortstop	**Dale Sveum**
Third Base	**Jim Lefebvre**
Outfield	**Joe Zdeb**
	Mike Krsnich
	Al Kvasnak
Catcher	**Doug Gwosdz**
Pitcher	**Eli Grba**

12

Best Quote
All-Star Team

First Base	**Dick Allen**	"If a horse can't eat it, I don't want to play on it." (1)
Second Base	**Frank Frisch**	"Oh, those bases on balls." (2)
	Larry Doyle	"Goddamn, it's great to be young and a Giant." (3)
Shortstop	**Leo Durocher**	"Do you want it, straight? Okay, back up the truck!" (4)
Third Base	**George Brett**	"Pressure? That's when you have to go to the unemployment office to pick up a check to support four people." (5)

Outfield	**Casey Stengel**	"Can't anybody here play this game?" (6)
	Willie Keeler	"Hit 'em where they ain't." (7)
	Willie Mays	"I don't compare 'em, I just catch 'em." (8)
Catcher	**Yogi Berra**	"It ain't over till it's over." (9)
Pitcher	**Satchel Paige**	"Don't look back. Something might be gaining on you." (10)

Best Quote
All-Star Team
Notes

(1) The talented breed improver is obviously referring to that universally despised—except by owners—abomination, Astroturf.

(2) As a not-always-articulate radio color man for the New York Giants of the late forties, an era during which the team broke the National League home run record but went nowhere—mainly because of a pitching staff that seemed determined to help opposing clubs break home run records—Frisch was notorious for his eternally repeated lament: "Oh, those bases on balls," as the Giants' scatter-armed hurlers kept walking in the runs. It was understandable, if maddeningly monotonous, since Frisch had been a manager, and bases on balls are possibly the major cause of managerial ulcers.

(3) This lovely line, coined by "Laughing Larry" Doyle, one of the better second basemen of his time (1907–1920), was interestingly a couple of generations later attributed to Tommy Henrich, who was quoted: "It's great to be young and a Yankee." Whether Doyle's line had become so familiar a part of the sports culture that Henrich was consciously and humorously switching it, or some wise-ass sportswriter was just making his own sly joke, I really don't know.

(4) "The Lip" 's alleged recommendation to then New York Giants owner Horace Stoneham, who had just hired Durocher away from the Dodgers, when Stoneham asked what needed to be done to make the Giants winners. The ensuing bloodbath saw six of the team's eight regular position players lopped from the team and shipped off to foreign parts, including such local favorites as Sid Gordon, Johnny Mize, and Buddy Kerr. Durocher went on to win two pennants and a World Series with *his* kind of Giants team, which would boast even more popular local heroes, the likes of Willie Mays, Alvin Dark, Sal Maglie, and Eddie Stanky.

(5) What a guy!

(6) Bemused Casey's rhetorical question to his pathetic Mets of the early sixties, as he observed the conglomeration of used-up veterans, far from ready rookies, and not very talented regulars displaying their shortcomings during a spring training workout early in the club's checkered history. Of course, Casey's best quotes could fill many a book—and have helped many a sportswriter ("My writers," he appropriately named them) fill a column on a slow news day. Other standard Stengelisms: "You could look it up"; "You're full of shit and I'll show you why." My personal favorite is Casey's admonition to a young left-hander named McKenzie, a Yale alumnus, as he took the mound against a tough lineup. "Pretend they're the Harvards," suggested Ol' Case.

(7) This ranks with "Say it ain't so, Joe!" as one of the two most famous sayings of baseball's historic era. That Keeler managed to follow his own advice is attested to by his numbers in the record books. This, of course, was in the dead-ball age before Babe Ruth applied his own formula to the problem of hitting 'em where they ain't, namely, the stands and bleachers.

(8) Remarked by Mays when asked to compare his unbelievable catch of Vic Wertz's huge drive into the deepest

part of the Polo Grounds' legendary 483-foot center-field reaches during the 1954 World Series against Cleveland (won by the Giants in four straight) to a previous play he'd made. That had been against the Brooklyn Dodgers, when he ran down a deep fly going away, then whirled to nab the tagged-up Billy Cox at the plate. That more or less started the legend of Mays's unique fielding greatness. It also, incidentally was the play to which then Dodgers manager Chuck Dressen, ever the skeptic, reacted by saying: "I want to see him do it again." And so the Say Hey Kid did, again and again and again for twenty-two years.

(9) I contend that Berra, far from being the semiliterate dum-dum that popular legend seems to have enjoyed stamping him, is a brilliant stylist of the English language. (Not to mention his pennant-winning percentage as manager—better than Connie Mack's, John McGraw's, or Casey Stengel's.) His statement here expresses, in the most concentrated form, a truism of profound import. It embraces the drama of late-inning comebacks, the honor of not giving up against impossible odds, the importance of never taking anything for granted. I compare it to Vince Lombardi's "Winning isn't everything, it's the only thing." That doesn't seem to make grammatical sense either, but like Yogi's line, its meaning is powerfully expressed and unmistakable.

(10) A couple of alternatives merit consideration: (a) Preacher Roe's reply to a newsman's question about his repertoire, "I got three pitches. My change, my change off my change, and my change off my change off my change." I don't know whether the sly left-hander of the great Brooklyn Dodgers teams of the late forties and fifties expected opposing batsmen to swallow that malarkey (Roe forgot to mention his sneaky fastball, nasty spitter, and pinpoint control), but he was always of the school that tries for a psychological edge, no matter how small its chance of success. (b) Dizzy Dean's conversation was richly larded with delicious localisms—his past tense of swing, for example, was "swang"—but his most memorable comment

has to be the one he made after a doubleheader in which brother Paul Dean had followed Diz's three-hit shutout with a no-hit game: "If I'da knowed Paul was gonna throw a no-hitter, I'da throwed one too." On another occasion, to a reporter's query about whether his toe had indeed been fractured by Earl Averill's line drive in the 1937 All-Star Game: "Fractured, hell—the damn thing's broke!" The damn thing was not the only thing broke; so was Diz's career. Then the outstanding pitcher in the game (you could look it up), Dean tried to come back prematurely, and in favoring the injury, destroyed his arm, effectively ending his dominance as the era's supreme power pitcher. He played out the string for a couple of years, throwing junk and employing guile, but the song was over, tragically.

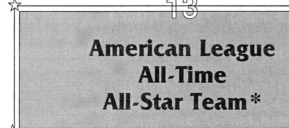

American League All-Time All-Star Team*

First Base	**Lou Gehrig**
Second Base	**Eddie Collins**
Shortstop	**Joe Cronin**
Third Base	**George Brett**
Outfield	**Babe Ruth**
	Joe Jackson
	Joe DiMaggio
Catcher	**Mickey Cochrane**
Pitcher	**Walter Johnson**

American League All-Time All-Star Team Notes

*Honorable mention: 1B—Jimmie Foxx, Hank Greenberg, George Sisler; 2B—Napoleon Lajoie, Lou Whitaker, Nellie Fox; SS—Luis Aparicio, Luke Appling, Tony Fernandez; 3B— Jimmy Dykes, Brooks Robinson; OF—Ty Cobb, Al Simmons, Tris Speaker, Ted Williams, Reggie Jackson; C—Bill Dickey, Yogi Berra; P—Cy Young, Lefty Grove, Bob Feller

National League All-Time All-Star Team*

First Base	**Willie McCovey**
Second Base	**Rogers Hornsby**
Shortstop	**Honus Wagner**
Third Base	**Mike Schmidt**
Outfield	**Willie Mays**
	Hank Aaron
	Frank Robinson
Catcher	**Roy Campanella**
Pitcher	**Christy Mathewson**

National League
All-Time
All-Star Team
Notes

*Honorable mention: 1B—Bill Terry, Orlando Cepeda, Johnny Mize; 2B—Frank Frisch, Billy Herman, Joe Morgan, Jackie Robinson; SS—Dave Bancroft, Ernie Banks, Arky Vaughan; 3B—Pie Traynor, Eddie Mathews; OF—Roberto Clemente, Stan Musial, Ralph Kiner, Hack Wilson; C—Johnny Bench, Ernie Lombardi, Gabby Hartnett; P—Sandy Koufax, Warren Spahn, Dizzy Dean, Tom Seaver, Carl Hubbell, Grover Cleveland Alexander

15

All-Time
All-Star
All-Star Team *

First Base   **Lou Gehrig**

Second Base   **Rogers Hornsby**

Shortstop   **Honus Wagner**

Third Base   **Mike Schmidt**

Outfield   **Babe Ruth**

                         Joe DiMaggio

                         Willie Mays

Catcher   **Roy Campanella**

Pitcher   **Christy Mathewson**

All-Time
All-Star
All-Star Team
Notes

*Of course, this is a matter of opinion, but I am willing to defend my selections while acknowledging the claims of alternative choices. Interestingly, except for first base, where such players as Jimmie Foxx and Hank Greenberg have to be considered worthy competitors, the other infield positions would seem to be incontestable. Hornsby, Wagner, and Schmidt are singularly superior to any pretenders at their positions. The rest of the team presents serious problems. After Ruth, who can confidently name a team that does not include Cobb, Mays, Aaron, DiMaggio, Speaker, Williams, Jackson, Mantle, Clemente, Musial, Kaline? As to catcher, how do you name one and ignore a group that includes Bench, Dickey, Cochrane, Campanella, Berra? Pitcher presents an even greater dilemma. Mathewson, Young, Johnson, Grove, Dean, Hubbell, Feller, Spahn, Koufax, Gibson, Seaver all dominated their eras. Oddly, the holder of some of baseball's most impressive records is not in my opinion eligible. Nolan Ryan, uncontested strikeout leader and pitcher of five no-hit no-run games, has never proven himself in the one category that counts most—the won-lost column. Conversely, Ewell Blackwell, the most overwhelming pitcher I have ever seen, had an injury-shortened career that disqualifies him from consideration.

16

All-Goat
All-Star Team

First Base **Bill Buckner (1)**

Second Base **Aaron Ward (2)**

Shortstop **Roger Peckinpaugh (3)**

Johnny Pesky (4)

Third Base **Heinie Zimmerman (5)**

Outfield **Fred Snodgrass (6)**

Hack Wilson (7)

Willie Davis (8)

Catcher **Mickey Owen (9)**

Pitcher **Ralph Branca (10)**

All-Goat
All-Star Team
Notes

(1) There have been few more dramatic turnarounds in sports history than the one caused by Red Sox first baseman Bill Buckner's muffing Met batter Mookie Wilson's ground shot down the first base line to let in the winning run in the sixth game of the 1986 World Series. All the elements of high drama were present—the Red Sox on the verge of finally atoning for their depressing history of World Series failure dating back nearly sixty years; the "arrogant" New Yorkers about to be put in their place by the scholarly gents from New England; Red Sox manager John McNamara on the verge of reclaiming his reputation as a winner after years of being kicked around the leagues. It was not to be. The unfortunate Buckner, insistent on playing despite his grotesquely injured leg (he must surely be regarded as nothing less than heroic and blameless considering the circumstances), was doomed to perennial purgatory in the scriptures of baseball goathood. (Buckner's designation as ALL-GOAT All-Star Team first baseman dislodges the most long-standing legendary goat in modern baseball history. Heretofore, New York Giants first baseman Fred Merkle stood tall as the original goat for his notorious failure to touch second base in the crucial game of the 1908 National League pennant race between the Giants and Cubs, ultimately costing the Giants the pennant.

(2) In the final game of the 1921 World Series, Yankees second baseman Aaron Ward walked with one out in the

bottom of the ninth and the Giants leading one to nothing. On a simple groundout by the next batter, Ward tried to go to third. Evidently he'd forgotten what a leaden-footed base runner he was. Instead of a man in scoring position with two out, the Yankees had lost a World Series.

(3) Washington Senators shortstop Roger Peckinpaugh engraved his name in the eternal goatskin scrolls by committing seven errors in the 1925 World Series against Pittsburgh. Ironically, Peckinpaugh won the American League MVP that same year. Go know.

(4) The highly popular and talented Johnny Pesky, anchor of the Red Sox infield of the late forties and early fifties, was designated the goat of one of the most famous foulups in Series history—Enos Slaughter's base-running coup, scoring from first base on a single in the '46 Series between the Sox and the Cardinals. As it happens, it was a bum rap. But the gentlemanly Pesky never bothered to defend himself against it. This would have meant shifting the blame to the true culprit, Sox catcher Roy Partee, who was not in position to take Pesky's throw, causing the latter's notorious hesitation until it was too late to catch the speedy Slaughter at the plate.

(5) Since he started his career with the Dodgers at third base, I hereby exercise my power over the authors of this book to name Gil Hodges third baseman of our ALL-GOAT All-Star Team. To earn this honor, Hodges went zip for 21 to contribute substantially to the Dodgers' losing effort against the Yankees in the 1952 Series. To buttress taking said liberty, I suggest that had the Dodgers not had the likes of Billy Cox and Jackie Robinson stationed at the hot corner, Hodges might have done even greater things at third than his extraordinary accomplishments at first. After all, he *was* a right-handed thrower. The other popular candidate for the position traditionally has been the infamous third base goat, Heinie Zimmerman of the New York Giants, frozen in baseball history in the act of futilely chasing White Sox second baseman Eddie Collins, one of the great base runners of all time, to home plate as Collins scored the run

that beat the Giants in the 1917 World Series. Actually, Zimmerman's goathood is similar to Pesky's in being wholly undeserved. He was chasing Collins only because his fellow infielders had committed the cardinal bonehead crime—failure to cover home plate.

(6) Giants outfielder Fred Snodgrass broke Christy Mathewson's heart when he dropped a fly ball in the tenth inning of the seventh game of the 1912 World Series between the Boston Red Sox and the New York Giants, with the Giants ahead by two to one. This, followed by a misplayed foul pop by first baseman Fred Merkle (my only double-dipper goat), led to Matty losing the game.

(7) Wilson was largely responsible for one of the most dismal records in World Series—and Chicago Cubs—history, the ten runs the team gave up to Connie Mack's powerhouse Philadelphia Athletics in a single inning of the fourth game of the 1929 World Series. When a fella loses two fly balls in the sun—in one inning—it's shocking how the runs can pile up.

(8) Speaking of fly balls, a key factor in the Orioles' sweep of the Dodgers in the 1966 World Series was Koufax's loss in game two. The Untouchable One was matching Jim Palmer's eventual shutout through five innings, when disaster struck in the person of Willie Davis, one of L.A.'s best players, among the fastest men and most skillful center fielders in baseball. Davis merely muffed two routine fly balls, inevitably leading to Koufax's rout. Chances are Baltimore would have won the Series anyway, since they won the final three games by shutouts (by Palmer, Wally Bunker, and Dave McNally). But had Koufax managed to sweat out his own shutout and a win for the Dodgers in that second game, it would have meant a second turn for him—in the fifth game—and a possible three-games-to-two situation instead of four down and out.

(9) One of the most famous goats for his misfortune in the 1941 Series, won by Yankees over the Dodgers, four

games to one. In the fourth game, with the Dodgers ahead four to three late in the game, two out and two strikes on Tommy Henrich, Hugh Casey's three-strike pitch got past Owen, putting Henrich on first. Giving that Yankee team a life was risky business. They rallied to win the game and shift the Series' momentum back where—in those days—it belonged. Poor Owen remains skewered in the Goat Pantheon even though it's been generally acknowledged for years that Casey's pitch that got by him was an uncatchable spitter.

(10) Branca gave up the most famous home run in baseball history, Bobby Thomson's line drive into the left-field lower deck of the Polo Grounds in the ninth inning of the 1951 National League playoff decider between the New York Giants and Brooklyn Dodgers. Since the Dodgers had already blown a thirteen-game lead in the final month of the season, there were plenty of other Dodger goats to share the blame for the team's monumental collapse. The unlucky Branca just chose the most dramatic moment to play his immortal part.

Abbott & Costello All-Star Team Notes

My source for this team, a recording of the famous "Who's on First?" comedy routine, does not, to my surprise, include a right fielder. No doubt, hordes of know-it-alls will arise to taunt me with the name of the missing player. So be it. I didn't promise you the *Britannica*.

I was not terribly shocked to discover that the routine was not original with Abbott and Costello. Burlesque comedians of the thirties—which Bud and Lou were—were not noted for respecting their competitors' rights of authorship.

Abbott & Costello
All-Star Team

First Base	**Who**
Second Base	**What**
Shortstop	**I Don't Give a Darn**
Third Base	**I Don't Know**
Outfield	**Why**
	Because
	??????
Catcher	**Today**
Pitcher	**Tomorrow**

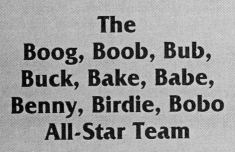

The Boog, Boob, Bub, Buck, Bake, Babe, Benny, Birdie, Bobo All-Star Team

First Base	**Boog**	(Powell)
Second Base	**Boob**	(McNair)
Shortstop	**Bub**	(McMillan)
Third Base	**Buck**	(Weaver)
Outfield	**Bake**	(McBride)
	Babe	(Ruth)
	Benny	(Kauff)
Catcher	**Birdie**	(Tebbetts)
Pitcher	**Bobo**	(Newsom)

19

Sons of All-Stars All-Star Team

First Base	**Dick Sisler, son of George**
Second Base	**Vance Law, son of Vernon**
Shortstop	**Hal Lanier, son of Max**
Third Base	**Buddy Bell, son of Gus**
Outfield	**Barry Bonds, son of Bobby**
	Chet Lemon, son of Bob
	Earl Averill, son of Earl
Catcher	**Terry Kennedy, son of Bob**
Pitcher	**Steve Trout, son of Dizzy**

Alcoholic All-Star Team

First Base   **Rudy York (1)**

Second Base **Billy Martin (2)**

Shortstop   **Rabbit Maranville (3)**

Third Base **Pie Traynor (4)**

Outfield   **Paul Waner (5)**

              Hack Wilson (6)

              Babe Ruth (7)

Catcher   **Rollie Hemsley (8)**

Pitcher   **Grover Cleveland Alexander (9)**

Alcoholic
All-Star Team
Notes

(1) Owns the only power record teammate Hank Greenberg doesn't monopolize in Detroit Tiger annals. York hit eighteen home runs in one month. Unfortunately, he also established the team—if not the league—record for absorbing booze. Unlike some others on our Alcoholic team, York's skills were affected by his habit, and his Hall of Fame potential was never realized.

(2) Never let it be said of the inventor of Billy Ball that he could hold his liquor. For Martin, alcohol was a magic potion that transfigured him into a sculptor bent on rearranging newly met drinking companions' faces. The fact that *he* led *Mickey Mantle* astray says it all.

(3) Nobody can figure out how this guy got into the Hall of Fame with his numbers, unless it was a tribute to his having stuck in the Bigs for over twenty years with a world-class hangover. Dick Bartell, a nondrinking shortstop who came up toward the twilight of Maranville's career, tells some good stories about "the Rabbit" 's boozing in his marvelous autobiography, *Rowdy Richard.* Such as the time in the mid-twenties when Maranville was honored with being appointed playing manager of the Cubs. He showed the seriousness with which he regarded his new responsibilities by getting tanked and by roaring through a Pullman

car in the middle of the night pouring ice water on his slumbering players. He also once said, "There is much less drinking now than there was before 1927, because I quit drinking on May twenty-fourth, 1927." I believe him.

(4) Traynor was one of those drunks who drive the temperance folks wild, by continuing to perform brilliantly for years after their livers should have been donated to science. A consistent .300 hitter and comparable to Brooks Robinson in the field, he may have been the best at the position during his era—the nineteen-teens to thirties.

(5) A class individual in every way, Waner was not one to revel in his drunkenness, à la the Maranvilles and Ruths, or to ignore it, as Traynor was able to do. He suffered pangs of remorse and humiliation the old-fashioned way, but the booze somehow did not prevent him from batting his way into the Hall of Fame. In fact, his may have been one of those cases of the addiction being an essential part of the machinery. It's claimed that on the few occasions when he was induced to stay on the wagon for short periods, he went into horrendous slumps. Then it was back to that pint of whiskey he consumed in the Pirates' dugout during the course of most games. According to Buddy Hassett, a good first baseman for the Dodgers and post-Gehrig Yankees, and onetime roommate with Waner on the Pirates, Waner's hangover cure was not totally orthodox. It consisted of doing fifteen backflips, by the end of which he was allegedly cold sober. Who could doubt any claim made in the name of this super-athlete?

(6) My choice for best apocryphal drunk story stars Wilson, whose monstrous numbers (e.g., 56 HRs and 190 RBIs in 1930) were posted in a pitifully drink-shortened career. "The Hacker" and his teammates, the oft-repeated story goes, were invited to attend a clubhouse lecture on the evils of alcoholism. To demonstrate his point, the lecturer placed a worm in a jar of water and another in a jar of alcohol. Sure enough, the worm in the alcohol stiffened and died, while the one in the water continued to swim around merrily.

"So," demanded the lecturer, triumphantly, "what does this experiment prove?" "It proves," allegedly replied Wilson, "if you drink water you'll get worms." It was obvious that Wilson spent most of his life in the denial stage of alcohol addiction. He always insisted, "I've never played drunk. Hung over, yes. But never drunk." Have it your way, Hack. But watch out for that water. You don't want to be coming down with worms.

(7) The Babe did not wind up in that Baltimore reform school by being a choirboy. The only temptation he was ever known to resist was the urge to let a high pitch go by. Many a day when "the Bambino" stepped into the batter's box, the catcher and umpire would be sent reeling from the alcohol fumes wafting out of his pores. So dominating was his influence, and so insidious was it considered by his employers during part of his Yankee career, that a $1,000 fine was imposed on any player caught out carousing with Ruth. Once, the Babe got loaded and decided to throw Yankees manager Miller Huggins off a train. It took several teammates to wrestle him down and prevent a serious accident. But there was a valid excuse. After all, Huggins had disagreed with Ruth on the proper pitching rotation for a series the Yanks had subsequently lost. All in all, Babe Ruth was the perfect personification of his time, the roaring twenties. If it was forbidden, he wanted it, and Prohibition was the law of the land. It's frightening to contemplate what the man might have accomplished had he stayed in shape. And who knows what part all that "Prohibition poison" he consumed might have played in his early death from cancer of the palate.

(8) For some reason, not too many catchers are on the all-time all-star drinking list, possibly because the job calls for highly responsible take-charge-type individuals. The position is important not only for the reason Casey Stengel gave, "If you don't have a catcher you get a lot of passed balls." Besides being the manager's surrogate on the field, a catcher must relate to and think along with the player who undoubtedly *is* the predominantly important player on the

team, the pitcher. All these considerations render the catcher the player least able to handle his many-faceted assignment with a lot of worms crawling around in his brain. Still, there have been some outstanding receivers who somehow managed to do the job while juggling major whiskey habits. Darrell Porter did it so well for so long, his entry into a drug and alcohol rehab program shocked a lot of baseball fans. Legends abound about Rollie Hemsley, one of the thirties' finest fielding catchers (he wasn't a bad hitter either). Dick Bartell, who roomed with him on the Pirates, recalls Hemsley strolling through a Pullman car tossing lighted matches into upper berths. As with many alcoholics, it didn't take much to get Rollie drunk. And as with many fighting drunks, it didn't take much to beat the hell out of him when he was loaded. Hemsley went the A.A. route in 1939 and cleaned up his act for good, to the surprise of many.

(9) So many pitchers are eligible for this team, it was tough to choose one. Some of the most notorious, drinkers like Rube Waddell and Bugs Raymond, bordered on the psychotic. Raymond, in particular, would stop at nothing in his foraging for drinks. One favored technique was to snatch drinks off other people's tables in restaurants. Raymond's promising career ended when, in the heat of a pennant race, Giants manager John McGraw summoned him from the bullpen to relieve Rube Marquard in a crucial game. When Bugs gloved an easy come-backer and flung the ball home instead of to first base, then staggered to the dugout, his relief stint and his career were effectively ended. Seems Bugs had grown weary waiting in the bullpen and had taken himself a little stroll out of the Polo Grounds to several saloons up the street on Manhattan's Eighth Avenue. A year later, he died in a flophouse in Chicago, at age thirty. Unlike Raymond, Waddell was another of those lucky drunks who can perform brilliantly despite a major habit. Connie Mack, who had managed numerous Hall of Famers (Eddie Plank, Chief Bender, and Lefty Grove among them) remembered him as the best pitcher he ever had. Waddell led the league in strikeouts six times, won twenty or more

games four times and nineteen twice. But he was out of the majors by age thirty-two and dead at thirty-seven. Bill James, author of the invaluable *Historical Baseball Abstract,* infers from contemporary accounts that Waddell was mentally deficient. There was Waddell's widely reported obsession with fires, which necessitated the constant close attendance of a teammate to keep Rube from dashing off in pursuit of every fire engine that wailed past the ballpark. Sam Crawford (Ty Cobb's Detroit teammate) many years later described how Tigers manager Hughie Jennings would distract Waddell from his game concentration by showing him little novelty toys. And it was well known that his wages would be doled out by concerned manager Connie Mack five or ten dollars at a time, for fear that any more cash in his pocket would finance a toot to parts unknown. (John McGraw, showing similar concern for Bugs Raymond, had his salary paid directly to his wife.) As stated before, drunken pitchers abound in the annals of the game. Dazzy Vance, Van Mungo, Don Newcombe, Bob Welch, all are well qualified for this team by virtue of their exploits with the ball and/or the bottle. I feel "Pete" Alexander rates it on the basis of his numbers and his longevity, remarkable for so confirmed a drunk. Considering that his manager routinely frisked him for concealed pints on his way to the mound (it was usually already too late), Alexander's sustained brilliance was remarkable.

Pollyanna
All-Star Team

First Base	**Alan Knicely**
Second Base	**Buddy Dear**
Shortstop	**Bobby Valentine**
Third Base	**Jake Virtue**
Outfield	**Wilbur Good**
	Earl Grace
	Bob Christian
Catcher	**Rick Sweet**
Pitcher	**Ron Darling**

Switch Hitter
All-Star Team

First Base	**Eddie Murray**
Second Base	**Frank Frisch**
Shortstop	**Ozzie Smith**
Third Base	**Jim Gilliam**
Outfield	**Mickey Mantle**
	Willie McGee
	Tim Raines
Catcher	**Alan Ashby**
Pitcher	**Vida Blue**

Native American All-Star Team (1)

First Base	**Rudy York (2)**
Second Base	**"Indian Bob" Johnson (3)**
Shortstop	**Louis Bruce**
Third Base	**John Leonard Roosevelt "Pepper" Martin (4)**
Outfield	**Louis F. "Chief" Sockalexis (5)**
	Jim Thorpe (6)
	Ernie "Chief" Koy (7)
Catcher	**John Tortes "Chief" Meyers (8)**
Pitcher	**Charles Albert "Chief" Bender (9)**

Native American
All-Star Team
Notes

(1) I have long suspected that many more players of American Indian descent have played major league baseball than the relatively few legendary ones, Thorpe and York and Bender. Surprisingly, even institutions like the Heye Museum of the American Indian keep no such records, although I am pleased to report that the nice lady who answered the phone at the Heye was able to inform me that her cousin Ken Berry, a damned good American League outfielder of the sixties and seventies, happened to be a full-blooded Potawatomi. Slowly, I gathered enough players to outfit a pretty solid lineup, in the process enjoying some delightful conversations with various authorities around the country. (I would like to thank especially Dr. Garold Holstine of Bacone College in Muskogee, Oklahoma, and Mr. Turner Cochran of the American Indian Athletic Hall of Fame for their kind help.) I still feel frustrated at my failure to find more of the many candidates I am convinced yet remain to be discovered. Still, the team assembled here is not too shabby.

(2) Rudy York, a good part Cherokee and all muscle, rapped out eighteen home runs in the month of August 1937, a record that has stood fast for five decades. York's well-publicized alcoholism (possibly too well publicized, thanks to its stereotypical aptness and the temptation to nod

knowingly at another Indian victim of "firewater") probably had a deleterious effect on his career. For each year from 1937 to 1943, when he reached age thirty, York averaged .286 and twenty-nine home runs. The next, and final, four full years of his career—two of them during wartime when an authentic star's stats would seem certain to improve— York averaged .262 and eighteen homers, ironically the same number he'd hit in that one magic August during his first full season in the majors. It is probable that this premature falling off prevented York's induction into the Hall of Fame.

(3) Because of a paucity of Native American infielders, it was necessary to switch one noninfielder—"Indian Bob" Johnson—to second base, a position he played a couple of dozen times—and nonshortstop Lou Bruce, a Mohawk utility infielder brought up for a cup of coffee by Connie Mack in 1904, to that position. (Mack, who had hit the jackpot with his brilliant Native American right-hander, Chief Bender, was evidently trying to get lightning to strike twice. It didn't, and Bruce was out of the majors after less than a full season.) Johnson, on the other hand, was a solid outfield performer for the White Sox and three other American League Teams for fourteen years. His brother, Roy, had a ten-year career almost equally fruitful. Oddly, the brothers had identical lifetime BAs—a very respectable .296.

(4) One of the most interesting cases, the legendary "Wild Hoss of the Osage" never, as far as I can determine, revealed his Indian heritage. The fiery competitor's Oklahoman background and his physical appearance strongly indicated that possibility. It was finally confirmed by the 1983 edition of the *Baseball Research Journal,* in an informative article, "The American Indian in the Major Leagues," by Stephen I. Thompson.

(5) Sockalexis, a Penobscot from Maine, played the outfield for Cleveland, then called the Spiders, from 1897 to 1899. A cultivated college graduate, he took Cleveland by storm in his first season, batting .338 and playing the out-

field artistically. Apparently even less able to handle his alcohol than York and Thorpe, Sockalexis (also nicknamed the inevitable "Chief") plummeted like a stone after that brilliant rookie season, and was out of baseball just two years later. In a remarkable statement, Hughie Jennings, Hall of Fame shortstop and manager, claimed his contemporary Sockalexis "should have been the greatest player of all time . . . greater than Cobb, Wagner, Lajoie, Hornsby and any of the other men who made history for the game of baseball . . ." Quite a mouthful, and about a man who played exactly ninety-three games in the major leagues. Talk about making an impression. In 1915, nearly twenty years after his short career in Cleveland, when the team finally decided on its present nickname through a fan contest, the name "Indians" was elected—in memory of Sockalexis.

(6) As possibly the most famous athlete in American history, Thorpe's tragic story, from the heights of his Olympic and football triumphs to the depths of the loss of his trophies, death of his son, and descent into alcoholism, is well known. Sadly, he did not live to see the restoration of his trophies to his family, although he was around to see Burt Lancaster play him in a filmed autobiography. (See also: FOOTBALL PLAYER, ALCOHOLIC All-Star teams.)

(7) In researching Native American major leaguers, I was surprised at the seeming total ignorance of the existence of Ernie Koy, an excellent player who came up with the Dodgers in the late thirties, to a clamorous welcome. I saw him a number of times in center field for the Dodgers. He could cover ground, was an excellent base runner, and though, as a twenty-nine-year-old rookie he did not have many years left to enjoy big league perks (a circumstance Koy shared with such other minority players as Chief Meyers, Benny Kauff, and George Stone), he made the best of his limited time in the Bigs, hitting .300 for the Cardinals after being traded there from Brooklyn. If the name sounds familiar at all, it can only be because his son, Ernie, Jr., enjoyed a few brief moments of moderate success as a running back for the New York football Giants in the early sixties.

(8) John Tortes Meyers—again the patronizing "Chief" nickname—was a splendid contributor to John McGraw's great New York Giants teams of the second decade of the twentieth century. A Cahuilla tribesman from California, Dartmouth man Meyers was doubtless better educated than most of his jock colleagues, who patronized or outright insulted him as an uncivilized savage. The fact that Meyers did not break in until age twenty-nine may well have prevented his induction into the Hall of Fame. Although he played for nine years, his best days were behind him when the masters of the game finally condescended to let him into their club.

(9) Bender, a Chippewa Sioux from Crow Wing County, Minnesota, and like Thorpe, a star athlete at Carlisle Indian School, is one of two identifiable Native Americans in the Hall of Fame. He won 210 games over a sixteen-year career in the big leagues, most of them with Connie Mack's Philadelphia Athletics. Bender was a stalwart on a staff that included two other Hall of Famers, Eddie Plank and Rube Waddell. The other Hall of Famer of known Indian descent, Early Wynn, won three hundred games in a twenty-three year career with the Senators, Indians, and White Sox, and was renowned for his tough-minded and tenacious approach to the business of pitching. Wynn personified the cliché "When the going gets tough, the tough get going." Rounding out the starting staff for the NATIVE AMERICAN All-Star Team is the brilliant part-Creek Allie Reynolds, achiever of two no-hit no-run games during his thirteen-year major league career with, first, the Cleveland Indians and then, much more important, with the Yankees during their extraordinarily fruitful stretch from 1947 to 1954. In that eight-year period the Yankees won six World Series (in which Reynolds posted a 7 and 2 record). A remarkable athlete, Reynolds starred for four years at Oklahoma A & M (now Oklahoma State) in track, football, and baseball, and recalls proudly the opinion expressed by Olympic wrestling coach Clarence Gallagher (then at Oklahoma A & M) that Reynolds was the greatest natural athlete he had ever seen. Others of Indian descent to make it as pitchers

in the Bigs include Cal McLish, winner of ninety-two games in fifteen years with six teams; Elon Hogsett, a relief specialist for Detroit's pennant-winning teams of the midthirties; and "Silent John" Whitehead, who somehow contrived to win forty-nine games with the pathetic White Sox and Browns of the thirties. Then we have the sad case of Euel "Monk" Moore, a promising right-hander who broke in with the Philadelphia Phillies in 1934. As told by Moore's Phillies teammate Dick Bartell in his *Rowdy Richard* autobiography, the team's manager, Jimmie Wilson, forced Moore to alter his pitching delivery, causing the damage to his arm that ended his career. It could stand as a symbol of the Native American's fortunes in our society.

24

Alliteration
All-Star Team

First Base	**Ham Hyatt**
Second Base	**Denny Doyle**
Shortstop	**Creepy Crespi**
Third Base	**Sibby Sisti**
Outfield	**Whitey Witt**
	Bingo Binks
	Kiki Cuyler
Catcher	**Duffy Dyer**
Pitcher	**Bush Bates**

(Not to mention Bock Baker, Boom Boom Beck, Bevo LeBourveau, Hub Hart, Hank Helf, Tim Teufel, et al.)

25

Rookie of the Year All-Star Team

First Base	**Willie McCovey**
Second Base	**Rod Carew**
Shortstop	**Cal Ripken, Jr.**
Third Base	**Dick (né Richie) Allen**
Outfield	**Andre Dawson**
	Willie Mays
	Frank Robinson
Catcher	**Johnny Bench**
Pitcher	**Tom Seaver**

Broadway/Hollywood All-Star Team (1)

First Base	**Gary Cooper (2)**
Second Base	**David Alan Grier (3)**
Shortstop	**Joe E. Pata (4)**
Third Base	**John Cusack (5)**
Outfield	**Levar Burton (6)**
	Tony Perkins (7)
	William Bendix (8)
Catcher	**Paul Winfield (9)**
Pitcher	**Ronald Reagan (10)**

Broadway/Hollywood
All-Star Team
Notes

(1) While numerous baseball movies and plays have been made, football seems to have dominated the theatrical sports scene during the thirties, the Golden Age of Hollywood. College football musicals, dramas, and comedies were a popular Hollywood genre then, whereas baseball films were rare until a spate of biographies started appearing in the forties. Then, Monte Stratton, Babe Ruth, Lou Gehrig, Grover Cleveland Alexander were all portrayed on the screen, with varying success. Prior to that time, only large-mouthed comedian Joe E. Brown, himself a former professional ballplayer, seemed to have much interest in bringing the national pastime to the silver screen. The talented clown made a couple of rollicking baseball comedies in the thirties, *Elmer the Great* and a wonderfully funny version of Ring Lardner's classic *Alibi Ike* that is long overdue for revival. In recent decades, until *Bull Durham* and *Eight Men Out,* the only fictional movies we can recall with baseball themes were Robert Redford's *The Natural* and *Bang the Drum Slowly,* a serious drama in which Robert DeNiro played a goofy catcher character with a fatal disease. Now, with the successes of *Bull Durham* and *Field of Dreams,* we can look forward to years of baseball farces, dramas, comedies, and tragedies on the big screen.

Interestingly, Ronald Reagan was the only movie star to act in both sports, playing baseball Hall of Fame pitcher

Grover Cleveland Alexander and, in football—who, class?
The Gipper, of course.

Baseball Bio Critique: Must see: *Pride of the Yankees.* Avoid
like the plague: *The Babe Ruth Story.*

(2)	Lou Gehrig	*Pride of the Yankees*
(3)	Jackie Robinson	*The First*
(3)	Pee Wee Reese	*It's Good to Be Alive*
(5)	Buck Weaver	*Eight Men Out*
(6)	Ron LeFlore	*One in a Million*
(7)	Jimmy Piersall	*Fear Strikes Out*
(8)	Babe Ruth	*The Babe Ruth Story*
(9)	Roy Campanella	*It's Good to Be Alive*
(10)	Grover Cleveland Alexander	*The Winning Team*

Name Ending in Ski
All-Star Team

First Base	**Ted Kluszewski**
Second Base	**Bill Mazeroski**
Shortstop	**Whitey Kurowski**
Third Base	**Jabbo Jablonski**
Outfield	**Rip Repulski**
	Greg Luzinski
	Carl Yastrzemski
Catcher	**Carl Sawatski**
Pitcher	**Stan Coveleski**

Triple Crown Winner All-Star Team

		HR	RBI	BA	YEAR
First Base	Lou Gehrig	49	165	.363	1934
Second Base	Napoleon Lajoie	14	125	.422	1901
Shortstop	Rogers Hornsby*	42	152	.401	1922
Third Base	Heinie Zimmer-man	14	103	.372	1912
Outfield	Ted Wil-liams	36	137	.356	1942
	Mickey Mantle	52	130	.353	1956
	"Ducky" Medwick	31	154	.374	1937
Catcher	Jimmie Foxx	48	163	.356	1933
Pitcher	Paul Hines**	4	50	.358	1878

Triple Crown Winner
All-Star Team
Notes

*While indisputably the greatest hitter ever to play second base (sorry, Nap), Hornsby started in the major leagues as a shortstop.

**I beat the game on a technicality. Hines, who played the outfield, first base, second base, and shortstop during a fifteen-year career in the (then) Bigs, pitched one inning for Providence of the National League in 1884.

Intimidating
All-Star Team

First Base	**Willie McCovey (1)**
Second Base	**Jackie Robinson (2)**
Shortstop	**Ozzie Smith (3)**
Third Base	**Mike Schmidt**
Outfield	**Ty Cobb (4)**
	Ralph Kiner
	Vince Coleman (5)
Catcher	**Johnny Bench**
Pitcher	**Nolan Ryan (6)**

Intimidating
All-Star Team
Notes

(1) McCovey, Kiner, Schmidt, and Bench have had one thing in common—the sense of impending doom they've inspired in the hearts of the opposition when coming to bat at a crucial point of a game. As a Giants fan, I well remember the feeling when Kiner would come up in a late inning—my team usually being involved in a pennant race, his Pittsburgh Pirates at historic depths of ineptitude except for him—knowing it was just a question of time before disaster struck. That dread sensation of waiting for the other shoe to drop was repeated later, with Willie McCovey, when I, like most loyal Giants fans, had finally faced the inevitable—the Giants were not coming back to the Polo Grounds—and had switched allegiance to the Mets. More than just the anticipation of the crushing home run blow was the brutal authority with which they punished the ball—the way they sent those monsters into orbit just seemed to rub it in even worse.

(2) Robinson's force of will was so overpowering, he generated the feeling that he could do whatever he wanted to on the field. His power seemed to be directed at his opponents in waves of energy that mucked up their gears. You knew he was going to steal the key base, get the big hit, make the great fielding play when it was needed—and there was no stopping him. Onetime St. Louis catcher Joe

Garagiola put it well, recalling the strategy discussions before the Cardinals would play the Dodgers. "We used to start with Jackie Robinson and the manager would say you gotta keep him close at first, then he would say you gotta keep him close at second, and then he would say you gotta keep him close at third because he likes to steal home. When you go over a guy base by base, you know you're in a lot of trouble."

(3) Ozzie Smith has the same effect on batters that the great power hitters have on pitchers. They know he's going to rob them, one acrobatic way or another, before the game is over. Like guards altering their trajectory to try to shoot over Kareem Abdul-Jabbar, batters try so hard to hit it where Ozzie ain't, it tangles up their swings, and probably has as much to do with his team's positive pitching stats as Whitey Herzog's fabled managerial genius.

(4) Cobb was frightening in many and varied ways. With a bat in his hand, that .367 number over twenty-four busy years made him the surest bet to hit your best pitch safely in the history of baseball. On the base paths, his penchant for slicing infielders to shreds with razor-sharp spikes is legendary. Off them, he was a vicious brawler, another devotee of the sucker punch, full of hate and venom. His aura is perhaps best summed up by longtime manager Connie Mack's nervous admonition to his Philadelphia Athletics: "Let him sleep, if he will. If you get him riled up he will annihilate us."

(5) Vince Coleman is an intimidating batter not because he is an intimidating batter but because he is a terrifying base runner. To sort that out, pitching to Coleman is not simply pitching to Coleman. It means pitching to a man who, if he gets on base, is sure to try to steal, and when he tries, is almost sure to succeed. It takes a pitcher with super mind control to blot that contingency from his head when he is facing Coleman. The extra pressure that this exerts on a pitcher affects his control to the point where Coleman is walked far out of proportion to his threat as a batter. Hav-

ing him on base then affects the pitcher's approach to getting the next batter out. In no time, the guy on the mound finds himself in deep trouble—and all because he is intimidated by a batter who hits fewer home runs than some pitchers.

(6) A tough choice because the position itself is the most intimidating of the nine. The pitcher is the only player who gets more than one hundred opportunities to murder or maim his opponents during the course of a game. I divide intimidating pitchers into three types. There are the sincere intimidators, truly ferocious individuals whose fierce hostility hits opponents as hard as their rocketing fastballs whiz by their chins. In this category I place Bob Gibson, who even scared his own catchers; Early Wynn, who once brushed back his fifteen-year-old son for hitting a long ball off him in a play situation; Dolf Luque, the hot-blooded Spanish don who once raced off the mound to the Giants' dugout and belted out outfielder Casey Stengel because the Giants' bench jockeying had gotten too abrasive. Then there are the "actors"—players who put on Oscar performances as tough guys to enhance their intimidation factor. Don Drysdale, Sal Maglie, Rhyne Duren, Goose Gossage, Burleigh Grimes, all avoided shaving between starts, banking on several days' growth of beard to exaggerate their menace. Drysdale thought nothing of chucking two successive dusters under a batter's chin; if it put him behind in the count, so be it. He had well-justified confidence in his control. Maglie, aptly nicknamed "the Barber" for his propensity to shave batters' faces closely with his high, hard one, glowered like a Barbary pirate on the prowl, while Grimes, last of the legal spitball pitchers (of whom onetime teammate Dick Bartell writes, "He made Bob Gibson and Don Drysdale look like the Angel of Mercy"), would have made a good stage director. He affected not only the unshaven look, but also the ugly uniform approach—his being always filthy and wrinkled. I remember seeing him at the tail end of his career, pitching relief for the Yankees in 1934. Even his stride to the mound was angry. He would glare in for his sign, and then bring the ball up to his mouth and proceed to slobber over it for what seemed like minutes.

By the time he sent it swimming to the plate, the batter didn't know whether to swing or call for a towel. I recall even the great Bill Dickey having trouble hanging on to that slimy mess. Rhyne Duren, to go with his blazing fastball, wore glasses thicker than the shot glasses he drank so much booze out of (he subsequently became an Alcoholics Anonymous counselor). Duren always made sure, when summoned into a critical relief situation, to start his warm-up with several wild heaves into the stands behind home plate. This did not encourage batters to stand in aggressively against his near-100-mph heater. As for Gossage, the following limerick by a witty friend says it all:

> Though they called Mister Gossage "The Goose,"
> He kept batters anything but loose.
> They were ever so fearful
> He'd give them an earful
> Of his one hundred m.p.h. juice.

Nevertheless, we have chosen Nolan Ryan for the honor of most intimidating pitcher—for several reasons. He doesn't derive help from a menacing personality, being rather laid back. He doesn't use gimmicks to gussy up a threatening appearance. All he's got is a 100-mph fastball, and a slight problem with control. That combination alone has cowed some of the toughest hitters in baseball history. As one of the latter, Reggie Jackson, put it succinctly—and frankly: "He's the only guy who puts fear into me. Not because he can get me out, but because he could kill me." Once an interviewer pointed out to Jackson that he was a renowned fastball hitter, and teased, "You should enjoy hitting against Ryan. You love fastballs." Reggie replied, "Yeah, and every kid loves ice cream—but not rammed down his throat by the gallon." In the words of Whitey Herzog: "Nolan has more effect on a team than any other opposing pitcher. That's because the players think about facing him the day before he pitches, the day he pitches, and the day after he pitches. On Monday they say, 'Oh shit, Ryan is pitching on Tuesday.' On Tuesday they say, 'Oh shit, look at his fastball.' And on Wednesday they say, 'Wow, did you see how fast he was?'"

Short
All-Star Team

First Base	JOE JUDGE	5'8"
Second Base	CUB STRICKER	5'4"
Shortstop	FRED PATEK	5'5"
Third Base	CHUCK DRESSEN	5'5"
Outfield	"WEE WILLIE" KEELER	5'4"
	ALBIE PEARSON	5'5"
	HACK WILSON	5'6"
Catcher	CLARENCE "KID" BALDWIN	5'6"
Pitcher	BOBBY SHANTZ	5'6"

**Drug Abuser
All-Star Team ***

First Base	ϑοε Πεπιτονε
Second Base	Αλαν Ωιγγινσ
Shortstop	Γαρρψ Τεμπλετον
Third Base	Παυλ Μολιτορ
Outfield	Δαῶε Παρκερ
	Ωιλλιε Ωιλσον
	Τιμ Ραινεσ
Catcher	Δαρρελλ Πορτερ
Pitcher	Δοχκ Ελλισ

*As they might appear to somebody who forgot to just say, "No!"

Drug Abuser
All-Star Team
Straight Version

First Base	**Joe Pepitone**
Second Base	**Alan Wiggins**
Shortstop	**Garry Templeton**
Third Base	**Paul Molitor**
Outfield	**Dave Parker**
	Willie Wilson
	Tim Raines
Catcher	**Darrell Porter**
Pitcher	**Dock Ellis**

32

Jewish All-Star Team

First Base	**Hank Greenberg (1)**
Second Base	**Buddy Myer (2)**
Shortstop	**Walter Weiss**
Third Base	**Al Rosen (3)**
Outfield	**George Stone (4)**
	Sid Gordon (5)
	Benny Kauff (6)
Catcher	**Johnny Kling (7)**
Pitcher	**Sandy Koufax (8)**

Jewish
All-Star Team
Notes

(1) Unquestionably the greatest Jewish position player and a Hall of Famer, Greenberg led the American League in home runs four times, RBI four times, bases on balls and doubles twice each, and runs and slugging average once each. His seasonal bests were eye-popping: 58 home runs (third best all-time), 183 RBI (third best all-time), 63 doubles, and .340 batting average. Interesting note: Greenberg became Ralph Kiner's mentor when he was traded to Pittsburgh early in Kiner's career, and there are remarkable coincidences in their lives. Each had his career drastically curtailed by years in the military during World War II and later by premature physical disabilities. Both, despite relatively modest home run totals of 300 plus—obviously due to lost seasons—were named to the Hall of Fame in recognition of their impact on the game, and both were among the most feared hitters of their times.

(2) The main difficulty in compiling a Jewish All-Star Team has always been the dearth of good Jewish middle-infielders. This has usually necessitated moving Buddy Myer, a Washington Senators second baseman of the thirties, and a true all-star, to shortstop and giving second base to Andy Cohen, a late twenties, early thirties "Jewish Hope" for New York Giants manager John McGraw, who never gave up on his dream of bringing a Jewish star to the Giants and capi-

talizing on New York's substantial Jewish population. Cohen, who broke in with a spectacular flourish, unfortunately proved to be a flash in the pan. Had McGraw survived and continued managing for a few more years, he would have had his Jewish star in the person of Harry Danning. A tough-hitting, good-fielding catcher, "Harry the Horse" (nicknamed for the Damon Runyon character, and for his undeniably longish face) played for the Giants in the late thirties and early forties until leaving for military service in World War II. As for the shortstop shortage, Walter Weiss, the Oakland As' 1988 Rookie of the Year, would appear to have solved that problem nicely. (It was thought to have been solved a generation ago with the emergence of the late George "Snuffy" Stirnweiss as a competent Yankee infielder—until a Jewish organization gave him its Jewish Sportsman of the Year award, whereupon Snuffy graciously informed them of his ineligibility on grounds he was a Christian. A similar situation arose in 1987, when hugely talented right-hander David Cone was traded to the Mets, and found himself getting lucrative offers to appear at the bar mitzvahs of numerous affluent thirteen-year-olds. Cone felt called upon to reveal that his name is a contraction of McCone, not of Cohen. Happily, this revelation did not seem to detract from Cone's popularity or the demand for his services at bar mitzvahs—for a reputed fee of $2,500 a shot.)

(3) Just a smidgen below Hall of Fame standard, 1953 MVP Rosen was the American League's all-star third sacker of his time, possibly the best in Cleveland's history. What he gave up to dynamic Indians predecessor Ken Keltner in the field, he made up for with his more potent bat.

(4) George Stone earns a spot on this team by being one of only two Jewish batting champions in baseball history, the other being second baseman Buddy Myer. As to trivia buffs declaiming, "Aha, what about Rod Carew?" Once and for all, Rod Carew is not Jewish, although that perception has endured through the years because his wife is. So persistent is the impression, Carew enjoys telling the story on

himself of the time he and Elliott Maddox, who does happen to be a convert to Judaism, got into a political argument with another player, who shall be nameless. Finally the other player threw down his hat in disgust, and snarled, "You damn Jews always stick together!"

(5) A hair more speed and Sid Gordon would have been a true all-star. He could hit, hit for power, field, and throw. But he lacked the fifth essential ingredient of the ideal player. Still, he put in a nice career with the Giants and Braves, was part of the Giants' team of Clydesdales who broke the record for home runs in a season in the late forties (John Mize, Walker Cooper, Willard Marshall, Bobby Thomson, among them). Along with most of those overweight blasters, Sluggin' Sid wound up in the shipment that new Giants manager Leo Durocher was intent on exporting when he advised owner Horace Stoneham to "back up the truck." Gordon and Marshall were included in the four-player package that made up the Giants' side of one of the important trades in their history. Coming to them in exchange were Alvin Dark and Eddie Stanky, heart and soul of the team's great pennant drive to catch the Dodgers in 1951.

(6) I love Benny Kauff. He was one of the game's most colorful players, and a tremendous talent who, like other "head cases," was unable to sustain his high level over the long haul. (One extenuating circumstance for the relative shortness of his big league career was that he was kept in the minors, which he burned up, long past the time he should have been called up—possibly because of the fairly widespread anti-Jewish attitudes that prevailed in baseball early in the century.) His most productive years were spent in the outlaw Federal League, which he easily led in batting twice, then a few .300-plus seasons with the New York Giants, after which a possible criminal streak diverted him from the game to more lucrative illegal pursuits. His career ended when the just-appointed baseball commissioner, the austere Kenesaw Mountain Landis, warmed up for the Black Sox by kicking Benny out of baseball in 1920 after he was

accused (but acquitted) of being part of a stolen-car ring. Benny would make the subject of a great Broadway musical.

(7) Johnny Kling (né Kline): first catcher to stand close behind the batter, and to throw out base runners from a crouching position. Starred for the Cubs from 1901 to 1911. With Roger Bresnahan, Kling was one of the two best catchers of the time. Half of the first all-Jewish battery, with Ed Reulbach. (Others: Sandy Koufax and Norm Sherry, Larry Sherry and Norm Sherry, Harry Feldman and Harry Danning)

(8) Any arguments?

33

W. C. Fields
All-Star Team*

First Base	**Fenton Mole**
Second Base	**Wayne Terwilliger**
Shortstop	**Rivington Bisland**
Third Base	**Urbane Pickering**
Outfield	**Earl Yingling**
	Aubrey Epps
	Liz Funk
Catcher	**Elmer Klumpp**
Pitcher	**Bob Giggie**

*For all those readers who, unlike the authors, have not seen every W. C. Fields movie forty or more times, you should be aware that all of his characters had outlandish names.

34

Remarkable Record
All-Star team

First Base	**Lou Gehrig**	2,130 consecutive games played
Second Base	**Rogers Hornsby**	Five-year average, 1921–25: .402
Shortstop	**Bill Wambsganss**	Unassisted triple play in 1920 World Series
Third Base	**Pete Rose**	4,256 career hits
Outfield	**Babe Ruth**	714 HRs after winning 94 games as a pitcher
	Joe DiMaggio	56 consecutive game hit streak

	Hank Aaron	**755 career home runs**
Catcher	**Moe Berg**	**Spoke 20 languages, including Japanese and Sanskrit**
Pitcher	**Johnny Vander Meer**	**Two consecutive no-hit no-run games in 1938**

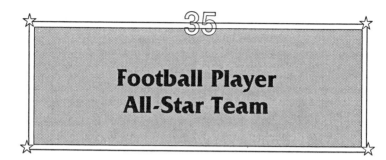

35

Football Player
All-Star Team

			YEAR GRADUATED
First Base	**Lou Gehrig (1)**	*Columbia*	**'25**
Second Base	**Jackie Robinson (2)**	*UCLA*	**'43**
Shortstop	**Alvin Dark (3)**	*S. W. Louisiana*	**'46**
Third Base	**Jim Davenport (4)**	*Southern Miss.*	**'54**
Outfield	**Jim Thorpe (5)**	*Carlisle*	**'12**
	Bo Jackson (6)	*Auburn*	**'86**
	Jackie Jensen	*U. Cal.*	**'50**
	Kirk Gibson (7)	*Michigan State*	**'78**

Catcher	**John Stearns (8)**	*Colorado U.*	**'73**
Pitcher	**Christy Mathew- son (9)**	*Bucknell*	**'03**

Football Player
All-Star Team
Notes

(1) Gehrig not only continued playing tackle for the Columbia football team for two years after joining the Yankees in 1923, he also kept playing baseball for the Lions. Oddly, his most notable college baseball feat was as a pitcher. He struck out seventeen Williams College batters in a game in 1925. That was the year he graduated and, to his credit, with his original class.

(2) Robinson (as previously noted, UCLA's first and only winner of varsity letters in four sports) was a tough running back and a good receiver. As a freshman in 1939, he was third leading rusher in the PAC 10 Conference. The following year, he was the conference's third leading scorer. Not bad for a guy with other things on his mind—like baseball, basketball, track, and a good scholastic standing.

(3) One of several All-American players on this team, Dark's football background was recalled in an incident involving him and his FOOTBALL All-Star Team middle-infield mate Jackie Robinson. The ferociously competitive Robinson, in his familiar style, bowled over the considerably smaller Giants second baseman, Davey Williams, in breaking up a double play. The stunned Williams had to be carried off the field. This infuriated Dark, the Giants' hard-muscled shortstop and, like Robinson, a former punishing running back. Almost in-

evitably, seemingly as if he had willed it, Dark tripled in his next at bat, and at the approach to third base, tossed a NFL-worthy flying block at Dodgers third baseman Robinson. The two fierce ex-footballers were dragged apart by quick-reacting umps to keep an ugly situation from turning really scary. Were there racial implications in this 1950s-era confrontation between the White Deep Southerner and the upwardly mobile assertive Black? Dark, a devout Christian and a strongly moral individual, should be given the benefit of the doubt as to his overt attitude. On the other hand, years later, as manager of the Giants, he was involved in another controversy when he remarked to a journalist friend, off the record, that some of his Hispanic players lacked hustle. Somehow the statement went on the record, to the profound embarrassment of Dark and the Giants management. But this was a tempest in a sangria glass compared with his subsequent ordeal at the hands of Charlie Finley, the George Steinbrenner role model of the sixties and seventies, who hired, fired, hired, and fired Dark to manage Finley's talented Athletics teams much in the manner of Steinbrenner *vis-à-vis* Billy Martin. But while the Yankees on again—off again odd couple nauseatingly persisted in professing deep affection for one another, Dark and Finley, refreshingly, have never made any secret of their mutual disdain.

(4) Davenport, the San Francisco Giants' fine third sacker of the late fifties and sixties, and their sometime manager, quarterbacked Southern Miss. in '53 and '54.

(5) The tragic history of Jim Thorpe would have excited Shakespeare. Never was a hero dashed from greater heights to sadder depths. The story is too famous to need detailed repetition here. What sports fan doesn't know about his single-handed defeat of Harvard, then football's great power, as leader of the Carlisle Indians college team? his incredible sweep of the 1912 Olympics' track and field events, comparable only to those, later, of Jesse Owens and Paavo Nurmi as individual explosions of dominance over all competition? the stripping of his Olympic trophies by the blue-

nosed bluebloods who then ruled American amateur sports when it was learned that Thorpe had earned a few badly needed dollars playing semipro baseball for a couple of summers? his gradual slide into alcoholic failure and his death without absolution or the return of his precious trophies from the U.S. Olympic powers? (Case in point, one Avery Brundage, a priggish snob and petty dictator, whose greatest claim to fame was kowtowing to Hitler during the Berlin Olympics of 1932 by having Marty Glickman, then an Olympic sprinter, scratched from the 400-meter relay to relieve Herr Hitler of the potential embarrassment of having to watch a Jew win an Olympic medal. Decades later, again in Berlin, it was Brundage who decreed that the games would continue on the very day that Israel's Olympic wrestling team was massacred by PLO terrorists.) Back to Thorpe. Though his baseball skills were mediocre—he could not hit the curve and his work habits were poor—Thorpe was employed by the New York Giants for parts of six years because the Giants' manager, John McGraw, was a publicity monster who appreciated the value at the turnstiles of Thorpe's tremendous notoriety. But the intense, tyrannical McGraw was not about to tolerate Thorpe's casual attitude toward rules and practice, and Thorpe, the proud and sensitive Sauk and Fox warrior, was not about to take any insults lying down. So the relationship was stormy, and McGraw expressed his irritation with his "head case" by sending him down to the minors frequently. The final breaking point was an apocryphal incident that could actually have happened, since it reflected the perpetual contest of wills between the two stubborn egotists. Allegedly, McGraw took Thorpe out of the lineup for a player Thorpe considered his inferior. When the player was injured, Thorpe, pinch-hitting, ostentatiously missed three straight pitches by a foot. McGraw traded him away the following season—Thorpe's last, incidentally, in the majors. Thorpe played pro football throughout his baseball career—in case Bo Jackson is interested. (Bo can't seem to hit the curve either. Must be something about pro football. Maybe Bo would do better swinging at an oval-shaped ball.) Later, in the mid-twenties, Thorpe played for the fledgling

New York Giants NFL team at age forty, again obviously being exploited for the promotional value of his still shining legend rather than for his long-faded skills at football, the game in which he had truly been a genius. Thorpe's Olympic trophies and medals were returned to his heirs long after his death and, I feel, more to salve the collective U.S. conscience than out of sincere regard for Thorpe, just another wronged Native American on our national scorecard.

(6) What more is there to say?

(7) I make Gibson and Jensen an entry. Their baseball careers would seem to be equivalent. Both won MVP. Like Gibson, Jensen was an overachiever who racked up very similar numbers. If Gibson breathes more fire into his teammates, Jensen was a better fielder. As for football, everybody knows about Gibson's recent career as a force at Michigan State. Jensen was better. He was a Jim Brown—type fullback at U. Cal. who would have had a shot at all-pro status in the NFL. On our FOOTBALL PLAYER All-Star Team, Jensen ranks at the very top in football greatness.

(8) Stearns would have been a high choice in the NFL draft as a defensive back, and the way things turned out for him in baseball, he probably should have chosen football. He spent ten years with the Mets when they were a fixture low in their division standings. For the last two of those years, he was disabled by a throwing-hand injury that effectively ended his playing career. Rubbing it in, as the unlucky Stearns was winding down with the Mets in 1984, the Davey Johnson era, the winningest in baseball, was being ushered in. Talk about your bad timing.

(9) Mathewson was better known for football than baseball during his Bucknell days. A bruising fullback (at six feet two inches he was considered unusually big for the times) and a skillful drop-kicker, he starred against a schedule that included some pretty strong squads (though not of the caliber of Ivy League colleges, then the powerhouses of

the game), Navy, Penn State, Army, etc. Mathewson left school in his junior year, 1902. Like Gehrig with the Yankees, Matty was signed with the Giants for two years before he quit playing amateur college sports—both interesting anomalies from the era of alleged pure amateurism.

Most Dramatic Clutch Performance All-Star Team

First Base	**Hank Greenberg (1)**
Second Base	**Bill Mazeroski (2)**
Shortstop	**Bucky Dent (3)**
Third Base	**Cookie Lavagetto (4)**
Outfield	**Bobby Thomson (5)**
	Kirk Gibson (6)
	Roger Maris (7)
Catcher	**Carlton Fisk (8)**
Pitcher	**Grover Cleveland Alexander (9)**

Most Dramatic
Clutch Performance
All-Star Team
Notes

(1) Greenberg's grand slam to clinch the pennant for the Tigers in 1945

(2) Mazeroski's ninth-inning homer in the seventh game of the 1960 World Series, to defeat the Yankees for Pittsburgh

(3) Dent's ninth-inning homer over Fenway's "Green Monster" in the 1978 American League East playoffs to beat Boston for the Yanks

(4) Lavagetto's double, as the Brooklyn Dodgers' third baseman, off the Yankees' Floyd Bevens in the 1947 World Series, to break up Bevens's bid for a no-hitter with two out in the ninth inning. It would have been the first ever World Series no-hitter.

(5) Thomson's "Shot Heard 'Round the World," his famous (or infamous if you were a Dodger fan) homer into the lower left-field deck of the long-gone Polo Grounds, off the Dodgers' Ralph Branca, in the third and final game of the postseason playoff series between the Brooklyns and the Giants for the 1951 National League pennant

(6) Gibson earned his spot on this team honestly when he outwilled the Mets in the 1988 National League playoffs. His twelfth-inning home run in the fourth game to prevent the Mets from taking a three-to-one lead in the series turned the momentum around and launched the suddenly charmed Dodgers' subsequent rush past the Mets and through the Athletics. Here again, it was Gibson who provided the cloak of invincibility for his not-that-gifted teammates when, too lame to start, he trumped forty–forty superman Jose Canseco's first-game grand slam with his own pinch homer to win that game and thoroughly psych out the young Oaklanders for the remainder of the Series. If ever an individual dominated a year's entire postseason doings, Gibson did.

(7) Maris broke Babe Ruth's record on the last day of the 1961 season. That's clutch hitting. Bear in mind that first he had to tie the Babe's sixty, another feat which had never been achieved. Lest we forget, Hank Greenberg and Jimmie Foxx, both legends all the way, had each hit fifty-eight homers in a season with several games to go, and had been unable to manage the final pair they needed for the tie. I happen to be one who does believe the asterisk next to Maris's achievement in the record book is proper. He had eight more games than Ruth, Greenberg, Foxx, or Hack Wilson had to compile his numbers. But we are talking about performing in the clutch, and when Maris needed those blasts to tie and then to break the record, he sucked it up and delivered like the true gentleman warrior he was.

(8) Fisk's twelfth-inning homer against the Reds in the 1975 World Series that tied the Series at three games apiece. Of course, in keeping with tradition, Boston proceeded to lose the seventh game.

(9) Grover Cleveland Alexander, a thirty-nine-year-old who liked his alcohol, struck out star rookie power hitter Tony Lazzeri with the bases loaded in the seventh game of the 1926 World Series, thus saving the Series for the Cardinals versus the Yankees of the "Murderers' Row" epoch. In an odd coincidence, both Lazzeri and Alexander were epilep-

tics in times when that ailment was considered a stigma. Lazzeri was fortunate in that he never experienced a seizure on the ballfield—the knowledge of which, the legend goes, encouraged the Yankees to sign him when other clubs, learning of his medical condition, hesitated.

37

Epithet
All-Star Team

First Base	**"The Earl Of Snohomish" (1)**
Second Base	**"The Fordham Flash" (2)**
Shortstop	**"The Hitless Wonder" (3)**
Third Base	**"The Wild Hoss of the Osage" (4)**
Outfield	**"The Splendid Splinter" (5)**
	"The Grey Eagle" (6)
	"The Reading Rifle" (7)
Catcher	**"The Duke of Tralee" (8)**
Pitcher	**"The Big Train" (9)**

Epithet All-Star Team Key.

(1)   Earl Torgesen

(2)   Frank Frisch

(3)   Leo Durocher

(4)   Pepper Martin

(5)   Ted Williams

(6)   Tris Speaker

(7)   Carl Furillo

(8)   Roger Bresnahan

(9)   Walter Johnson

Runs Batted In (Season) All-Star Team

First Base	**Lou Gehrig**	184
Second Base	**Rogers Hornsby**	152
Shortstop	**Vern Stephens**	159
Third Base	**Tommy Davis**	153
Outfield	**Hack Wilson**	190
	Hank Greenberg	183
	Babe Ruth	171
Catcher	**Jimmie Foxx**	175
Pitcher	**Wes Ferrell**	32

Fighter
All-Star Team

First Base	**Art Shires (1)**
Second Base	**Billy Martin (2)**
Shortstop	**Leo Durocher (3)**
Third Base	**George Moriarty (4)**
Outfield	**Ty Cobb (5)**
	Hack Wilson (6)
	"Ducky" Medwick (7)
Catcher	**Clint Courtney (8)**
Pitcher	**Dolf Luque (9)**

Fighter
All-Star Team
Notes

(1) Shires could hit baseballs almost as hard as teammates and opposing players, but he lasted only five seasons in the majors (mainly with the sad sack White Sox of the late twenties), thanks mostly to a huge chip on his shoulder—his head. Shires's concept of player-manager relations, for instance, was highly original, a point with which we are sure his onetime manager, Lena Blackburne, would heartily concur. Shires knocked Blackburne out three times in one season. It could hardly be handicapped as a fair match, since Shires was a professional-caliber boxer who had posters printed and a robe embroidered designating himself "Art the Great." He actually tried to promote a match between himself and Hack Wilson for the title of "Toughest Ballplayer," a project quickly aborted by Commissioner Landis, who was strict about preserving the dignity of the great national pastime. A more suitable contest between Shires and Wilson for the title of "Dumbest Ballplayer" would undoubtedly have ended in a draw.

(2) Everybody knows Jimmy Piersall was emotionally disturbed, but it took the inventor of Billy Ball to devise a therapy to tranquilize him effectively. Two right hands to Piersall's head did wonders in calming him down, indeed to the point of stretching him out in the vicinity of second base. But it seems to be pitchers who have always vexed Billy beyond

endurance. This predilection caused him to put left-hander Jim Brewer into the hospital. Proving he was not bigoted against lefties, he was later responsible for twenty stitches in righty Dave Boswell's face. His affair with Ed Whitson is dealt with in Note 9. As for the marshmallow salesman, I don't blame Billy. He probably got stuck with a bad marshmallow at some wienie roast or other.

(3) A notorious devotee of the "Sunday" (short for Sunday punch, now known as the sucker punch), Durocher was an artist at lulling a victim into relaxing his vigilance, then, *pow!*, right on the button. Like other sweethearts of the diamond—the Cobbs, McGraws, Medwicks, *et al.*—the Lip did not confine his aggression to his fellow players. In his most notable set-to, Durocher brutally thrashed an obstreperous fan under the Ebbets Field stands, allegedly with the assistance of a 270-pound security guard and a pair of brass knuckles. For what it's worth, without passing any value judgment, tough guy Durocher was declared 4-F in World War II because of punctured eardrums.

(4) Unsung, maybe the toughest of them all, Moriarty, as a Detroit teammate of Ty Cobb's in the early years of the century, is one of the few known to have not only defied the all-time bully's intimidation, but to have gone under the stands with Cobb and beaten the tar out of him. Twenty years later, retired to umpiring in the American League, Moriarty was attacked by four White Sox players in the umps' locker room at Comiskey Park. After a fairly long interval, the fight was broken up by the police—to prevent permanent damage to the Sox players—two of whom, catchers Charlie Berry and Frank Grube, had been college football stars.

John McGraw, who was instrumental in forging the reputation for excessive aggression of the old Baltimore Orioles, had a hair-trigger temper and the fighting ability to back it up. In the words of legendary sportswriter Grantland Rice, "[McGraw's] very walk across the field in a hostile town was a challenge to the multitude." Once, against the New York Giants, McGraw put two players into the hospital on a single play. After seriously spiking second baseman Monte Ward in the leg, he continued around the bases and spiked catcher Duke Farrell in the stomach while gouging his eyes. McGraw's own playing career was cut short, and effectively ended before his thirtieth birthday, in a triumph of poetic justice. Tigers outfielder Dick Harley, enraged at being spiked by McGraw, exacted vengeance the following day. Approaching third base, Harley launched his razor-sharp spikes at McGraw's knees in a furious slide. Muggsy's badly hemorrhaging knee was dreadfully torn. Beyond healing, the injury would permit him only some seventy-odd more games as an active player.

While he can hardly be ranked in viciousness with his tougher forerunners at the position, the normally sunny-tempered Ray Knight has on more than one occasion belted out an offending opponent, as Eric Davis would hasten to affirm. He's not really mean, it's just that he happened to have been an amateur boxing champ, and these young punks *would* try to take advantage of his good nature. Hell, we needed at least one God-fearing, churchgoing goody-goody on the team. It can get kind of depressing dealing with some of the characters in this crew.

(5) "When I began playing the game," Ty Cobb once said, "baseball was about as gentlemanly as a kick in the crotch." Let the record show the cuddly ol' Georgia Peach did his best to make matters worse. Freud would no doubt have found fertile grounds in Cobb's early background for his continual state of rage—his mother had killed his father—and he was perhaps conferring approval on this violent act by symbolically murdering everyone in his path. On the other hand, maybe he was just one mean sumbitch with an over-whelming urge to prove he was number one. According to onetime major league catcher and manager Paul Richards, Cobb's roommate in the minors, old Dodgers pitcher Nap Rucker once told Richards, "Ty fought and scratched and scrambled to be first, whether it was going to bed first or taking a bath first or getting to breakfast first . . . Cobb had an obsession about being first." He did achieve several firsts, including first in lifetime batting average, first in number of batting championships, and, as inarguably the most

hated man ever to play the game, first in the bile of his countrymen. As the following story indicates, he was definitely not first in compassion for the handicapped. It seems a Yankee fan named Claude Lucker made the mistake of heckling Cobb too vociferously for the future charter member Hall of Famer's liking. Cobb tracked him down in the stands and brutally beat, kicked, and spiked him. Lucker, hampered by childhood injuries to his hands that rendered them useless, was helpless to defend himself. When a bystander pleaded, "Don't kick him, he has no hands," the softhearted Georgia Peach allegedly responded, "I don't care if he has no feet!" Not surprisingly, Cobb did not spend his golden years being warmed by the companionship of his former colleagues. Roger Peckinpaugh (best remembered as the shortstop who committed seven errors in a World Series—the same year he won the MVP) recalled, "Nobody liked Cobb, including his own teammates. . . . We were in New York for an old-timers' game once. . . . Cobb wanted to buy the boys a drink, but they wouldn't take one from him." Cobb once told Paul Krichell, the great Yankees scout, that he would give up everything he had if the fellows he played with and against would only accept him and talk to him. But it was too late. He had gone too far too many times.

(6) The ol' Hacker earned his place on the FIGHTER All-Star Team by kayoing two Cincinnati pitchers on the same day. During that day's game, he objected, with his fists, to Ray Kolp's jockeying from the bench. That evening, when both teams were at the Cincinnati train station to embark on road trips, Wilson was accosted by a group of Reds eager to make him atone for that afternoon's transgression against one of their own. When the Reds' ringleader, pitcher Pete Donohue, was knocked on his keister by the egregiously annoyed fireplug who walked like a man, drank like a fish, and hit like a tornado, the uprising was ended—mercifully for the Cincinnati pitching staff (which had been more than sufficiently decimated for one day).

(7) Medwick hailed from Carteret, New Jersey, in those days teasingly referred to by New Yorkers as "the garbage cap-

ital of the world"—but not within earshot of the formidable Ducky. Among his many very short fights (one or two Medwick right hands were usually enough to end all hostilities): He punched out pitcher Tex Carleton, his Cardinals teammate, for holding him up at the batting cage; he cold-cocked journeyman Cards right-hander Ed Heusser right on the pitching mound, for questioning his hustle on a fly ball that fell for a hit; he belted out future syndicated columnist (then sportswriter) Irv Kupcinet, as his contribution to a heated discussion between Kup and Medwick's teammate, Dizzy Dean. Speaking of Dean and Kupcinet, the latter was witness to Dean's assault on another journalist, New York *Daily News* sportswriter Jack Miley, who had incurred the great Diz's ire by something he'd written about him. "I ain't takin' none of that crap from a $125-a-week writer," announced Dizzy. As I recall the press coverage of the incident, Miley was flattered by the amount, but not amused by the attack, which included being hit on the head with a pair of cleats. Miley happened to be about a foot shorter than Dean, but since when has bullying become socially unacceptable in professional sports? Incidentally, it was Dean who provided the definitive comment on Medwick as fighter. "Joe whops you and the fight is over," complained Diz. "That ain't no way to fight." True enough. That kind of thing could have cut some of John Wayne's longest scenes down to cameos.

(8) Courtney was definitely an exception to the rule of catchers being levelheaded field generals who keep their heads when all others around them are losing theirs. A hothead verging on the psychotic, Courtney was one of the few at the time who could hold his own with his opposite number, madman Billy Martin. I believe their two bouts ended in draws. Many catchers could probably make the FIGHTER All-Star Team if not constrained by their role as field leader. They are usually big, solid, aggressive, and brave about being barreled into by plate-frenzied baserunners. One who did once lose control was Bill Dickey, the great Yankee Hall of Famer. He broke Senators outfielder Carl Reynolds's jaw in two places as a sign of displeasure with Reynolds's manner of bowling him over at home plate.

(9) There seems to be agreement among his contempo-
raries that Luque was the toughest hombre ever to toe a
mound or graze a hitter's whiskers. This Cuban terrorist didn't
need a ball if some offender needed to be thrown at. He
once threw a knife at a teammate who slurred his Hispanic
accent. The fact the guy survived proves Luque only in-
tended it as a brushback, because he may have had the
best control in baseball at the time. Dick Bartell tells the
story, beautifully, of a bench-clearer between the Giants and
Cardinals when Luque was the Giants' pitching coach. Cards
infielder Don Gutteridge, then the fleetest base runner in
the league, was the first man out on the field, as Bartell
recalls the event. "He was so fast he ran straight into Dolf
Luque's fist. Down went Don like a sack of bricks." If Luque
had a weakness, apparently it was identifying voices. Once,
during his prime years as a starter for Cincinnati, his rabbit
ears picked up some particularly objectionable jockeying
from the Giants' bench. The stereotypically "hot-blooded
Latin" marched over to the bench and knocked out Casey
Stengel. It turned out that it had not been Casey who'd
been doing the jockeying, but that was okay. Stengel had
been such a maddening genius of the bench-jockeying art
for so long, in this case he was simply the boy who had
cried wolf.

   I can't close out this section without a tribute to Ed
Whitson. Normally an inoffensive country-boy type, Whitson earned his spurs by punching out the lights of one of
his most belligerent FIGHTER All-Star Team teammates,
second baseman Billy Martin. Thus, Whitson shares the only
two known decisions against Martin with that gin-mill wall
in Dallas.

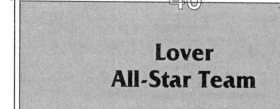

40

Lover
All-Star Team

First Base	**Steve Garvey (1)**
Second Base	**Burgess Whitehead (2)**
Shortstop	**Leo Durocher (3)**
Third Base	**Wade Boggs (4)**
Outfield	**Joe DiMaggio (5)**
	Babe Ruth
	"Turkey Mike" Donlin
	Dave Winfield
Catcher	**"King" Kelly (6)**
Pitcher	**Bo Belinsky (7)**

Lover
All-Star Team
Notes

(1) Garvey, having maintained a public image throughout his career as the quintessential Goody Two-Shoes of baseball, detonated a bombshell with the announcement that he was settling not one but two paternity suits simultaneously. If this doesn't rate first-string status on the LOVER All-Star Team, I'll eat my copy of *The Baseball Encyclopedia.* (Which might not be so difficult actually; I've already swallowed so much of it while researching this book.) Had Garvey's evidence of wholesale womanizing not suddenly exploded on the scene, this position would have belonged to Eddie Waitkus. After all, no greater love hath a man for his fellow woman than to get shot by her. That's what happened to Waitkus, a good-hitting first baseman for the Cubs of the late forties and early fifties, who accepted a young lady's invitation to visit her hotel room and was greeted by a few bullets in the abdomen. He survived, but never realized his potential, undoubtedly a result of the physical damage wrought by the shooting. If the story rings a bell, it's because Bernard Malamud used a similar incident as a crucial event in his novel *The Natural,* from which Robert Redford's movie was made. In a situation uncannily similar to the Waitkus incident, an earlier Chicago Cub, shortstop Billy Jurges, was shot in the stomach by a young lady who had been intimate with him, on the apparently mistaken grounds that this ploy would result in marriage. She ex-

pressed her disappointment through the barrel of a gun, but since, as everybody knows, only the good die young, the unpopular if talented young shortstop survived to play another ten years or so. Whatever became of the young woman who fanned on her attempt at high-caliber wooing, or why the Chicago Cubs are susceptible to this particular misadventure, I do not know. I do know they are not making groupies like they used to

(2) Whitehead, a brilliant-fielding, fair-hitting second baseman who played in three World Series during the thirties (with the Cardinals and the Giants), lost sixty points of batting average the season he (according to gossip of the time) went to bat against Tallulah Bankhead, one of the more notorious femmes fatales of American theater legend. The combination of Bankhead and the advent of World War II effectively annihilated Whitehead's career by age thirty-one. Possibly to prove that her affair with baseball was not just a one-night stand, La Bankhead remained true to the New York Giants all her life. In fact, she is responsible for one of the more provocative quotes by a nonplayer: "There have been two geniuses—Willie Mays and Willie Shakespeare."

(3) Durocher always lived high on the show-biz hog, eventually spending more time with the nobility of Hollywood than with the baseball crowd. One of a fair number of big leaguers who pursued movie queens, Leo was for a time wed to Laraine Day, a big box-office draw of the forties. In an age when Hollywood stars were venerated, Leo moved among them as their social equal. Later, during a sort of semiretirement gig as a coach of the L.A. Dodgers, he filled the same role that Tommy Lasorda does today as Hollywood's liaison to the big leagues. Of course, the usually rotund strategist is not the type who could ever replace Leo in the hearts—or beds—of the ladies of the silver screen. Aside from Tommy's unswashbuckling girth, he's got the old-fashioned notion that an actress's place is in the kitchen, whipping up a kettle of *pasta e fagioli.*

(4) Margo Whatsername. Need we say more?

(5) Despite his shy demeanor, DiMaggio's actions obviously spoke louder than words. Judging from the evidence, his nickname "Joltin' Joe," could have described more than his doughty feats on the ballfield. Few recall that even before he stunned the world by sweeping Marilyn Monroe off her photogenic feet, he was renowned as a stud who favored showgirl types. His first wife, Dorothy Arnold, was another such starlet type.

Ruth, notorious for his gargantuan appetites for every source of pleasure, ate, drank, and loved with the same insatiable lust as he displayed for pitches to launch out of American League ballparks. It's been claimed by former teammates that the Babe once took on an entire brothel during one road trip to St. Louis. As for that famous "bellyache" that sidelined Ruth for nearly half the 1925 season, the general understanding has been that the ache was centered in a location somewhat lower than his belly—that in fact his ailment was a venereal disease.

Speaking of which, Dave Winfield well earned his place on the LOVER All-Star Team when he was sued by Ruth Roper (Mike Tyson's once—and possibly future—mom-in-law) for allegedly infecting her with gonorrhea. One might say that Dave likes to do unto others what George Steinbrenner tried for years to do to him.

A personal favorite is "Turkey Mike" Donlin of the early New York Giants—in his prime one of the best players of the era—who not only wooed and won a vaudeville performer named Mabel Hite, but gave up baseball for three full seasons (1907, '09, and '10) to pursue a career (and the ladies) in vaudeville and Hollywood. Donlin can actually be seen playing a Union general in Buster Keaton's silent-screen comedy masterpiece about the Civil War, *The General.* It was "Turkey Mike" who, when night baseball was introduced in the minors, lamented, "Jesus! Think of taking a ballplayer's nights away from him!" John Montgomery Ward was a New York Giants superstar and Frank Merriwell type of the 1880s and '90s. In the course of his seventeen-year career, Ward pitched, played second, third, short, and the outfield when he wasn't trying to integrate the National League and organizing a forerunner to the Players' Association. In his spare time, he hogged the headlines with his intense courtship of a beautiful Broadway star of the day named Helen Dauvray, née Ida Louise Gibson. Ida Louise, or Helen, evidently had an eye for publicity that Madonna—or even Margo Adams—might envy. She conceived the idea of a silver cup—named, lest anybody forget whose idea it had been, the Dauvray Cup—to be presented to the winner of the World Series (the second-ever Series was to be played between her sweetie's New York Giants and the St. Louis Browns in 1887). To give the devil his (or her) due, Ida Louise didn't dump Ward once he'd served her purpose. They were wed and lived happily ever after—or at least until their divorce eleven years later.

(6) Mike "King" Kelly, one of the first great media heroes of baseball, scandalized nineteenth-century fans by his involvement with music-hall star Maggie Cline, described in the press as "a buxom young lady." The greatest base runner of his time, starring for the Chicago White Stockings, Kelly is said to have originated the hit-and-run play, and he was the Kelly for whom the song "Slide, Kelly, Slide" was written in 1888. It was recorded by his inamorata, the aforementioned Ms. Cline. According to Noel Hynd, author of the definitive history of the New York Giants, *The Giants of the Polo Grounds*, the song "was a chartbuster in 1888." The lyrics, as recorded by Hynd:

Slide, Kelly, slide!
Your running's a disgrace!
Slide, Kelly, slide!
Stay there, hold your base!
If someone doesn't steal you,
And if your batting doesn't fail you,
They'll take you to Australia,
Slide, Kelly, slide!

A bit more rhetorical elegance and it might reach the level of a rap lyric.

(7) Bo Belinsky tops the list of skirt-chasing pitchers largely because he played in L.A., where he climbed on the show-biz hype machine and rode it to publicity heaven. Being discovered by Walter Winchell, a sports illiterate with a nose for future celebrities, didn't hurt. Neither did his romance with Mamie Van Doren, the Madonna of her time (in her gift for self-promotion, not in talent). How much Mamie contributed to Bo's meteoric fall—it seems one day he was pitching a no-hitter, and before you could say flash-in-the-pan, his career was over—nobody can say. No doubt Mamie contributed some big league distraction, but Bo was obviously a born-to-lose hellion with a self-destructiveness that didn't need any help. When he finally split with Mamie, Bo, ever the gentleman, graciously commented, "I need her like Custer needed Indians."

Rube Marquard, the famous "$11,000 Lemon" (the epithet he was plastered with after the Giants bought him for that sum, and he initially failed to fulfill expectations) who went on to set the still-standing major league record of nineteen straight wins in a season, was a naughty fellow with matinee idol looks. He stole Broadway star Blossom Seeley from her husband and after much hanky-panky, married her.

My favorite pitching stud was Van Lingle Mungo, the hulking pitcher for the Bad News Brooklyn Dodgers of the thirties, who threw incredible smoke at opposing batters and a long lineup of assorted women. A former teammate swears that the following happened when Mungo's wife confronted him with a perfumed love letter from a strange lady addressed to him. Indignant in his wronged innocence, he insisted, "It must be for some other guy named Van Lingle Mungo."

41

Home Run Hitter (Season) All-Star Team

First Base	**Hank Greenberg**	**58**	**(1938)**
Second Base	**Davey Johnson**	**43**	**(1973)**
Shortstop	**Ernie Banks**	**47**	**(1958)**
Third Base	**Mike Schmidt**	**48**	**(1980)**
Outfield	**Roger Maris**	**61!**	**(1961)**
	Hack Wilson	**56**	**(1930)**
	Mickey Mantle	**54**	**(1961)**
	Ralph Kiner	**54**	**(1949)**
Catcher	**Jimmie Foxx**	**58**	**(1932)**
Pitcher	**Babe Ruth**	**60**	**(1927)**

!(This is not an asterisk.)

42

Home Run Hitter (Career) All-Star Team

First Base	**Frank Robinson**	**586**
Second Base	**Rogers Hornsby**	**301**
Shortstop	**Ernie Banks**	**512**
Third Base	**Harmon Killebrew**	**573**
Outfield	**Hank Aaron**	**755**
	Willie Mays	**660**
	Mickey Mantle	**536**
Catcher	**Jimmie Foxx**	**534**
Pitcher	**Babe Ruth**	**714**

Foot-in-Mouth All-Star Team

First Base	**Bill Terry**	"Is Brooklyn still in the league?" (1)
Second Base	**Jerry Coleman**	"He slides into second with a stand-up double!" or "Next up is Fernando Gonzalez, who is not playing tonight." or "There's a hard shot to Le Master—and he throws Madlock into the dugout!" (2)
Shortstop	**Leo Durocher**	"Nice guys finish last." (3)
Third Base	**Wade Boggs**	"One-night stands are ac-

		ceptable, but two-year affairs are not." (4)
Outfield	**Darryl Strawberry**	"Mex had his head up his ass, Kid gave up, and Nails was playing for himself." (5)
	Ralph Kiner	"Rookie Wilson could win the Mookie of the Year award." (6)
	George Foster	Was quoted in a way that implied his Mets bosses had racist policies. (7)
Catcher	**Yogi Berra**	"I thank everybody for making this day necessary." (8)
Pitcher	**David Cone**	"Jay Howell reminds me of a high school pitcher." (9)

Foot-in-Mouth
All-Star Team
Notes

(1) Terry's famous response to the press when asked if he was concerned about his Giants' last series of the 1934 National League season against their despised traditional rivals, the Dodgers. At the time, the Giants, the previous year's World Series champions, were tied for the lead with the Cardinals, with two games left in the season. Of course the snide crack got wide circulation, and of course the lowly Dodgers proceeded to beat the Giants and knock them out of the pennant. That would remain the high point of the decade for the Brooklyn "Faithful," as their passionate followers were known. Terry went on to win two more pennants as skipper of the Giants, who earned the dubious distinction of being the only team in the thirties to face the DiMaggio-Gehrig-Dickey-Ruffing-Gomez Yankees in a World Series without being swept.

(2) We could go on and on with Jerry Coleman's bloopers. As play-by-play guy for the San Diego Padres, he is uncontested champion of the world. Still, Coleman was an excellent player at second base for the Yankees. Of course, if baseballs were words, he would never have thrown to the right base.

(3) The fact that Leo the Lip—or "Lippy," as he was known during his playing days—finished last only once in twenty-

four years of managing in the major leagues would seem to confirm his oft-quoted truism.

(4) Boggs's profound philosophy of marital fidelity, as expressed by him after baseball groupie Margo Adams went public about their four-year liaison. Boggs has since apologized to his teammates, his family, his employers, his fans, and for all anyone knows to the editor of *Penthouse* (which ran Adams's story of the affair). To date, none of the above has publicly accepted his apology (although his wife did appear with him on *20/20* for a Barbara Walters interview). And Margo Adams didn't call off her palimony suit either. Some days you just can't buy a hit. Actually, of course, that doesn't apply to Boggs, who can't remember the last day he couldn't hit 'em where they ain't.

(5) In an interview with respected New York *Daily News* sports columnist Mike Lupica for *Esquire* magazine, in which the self-styled "Straw that stirs the drink" blamed teammates Keith Hernandez, Gary Carter, and Len Dykstra—three of the most intensely competitive players in baseball—for the Mets' failure to win their division in 1987. Naturally, when the story appeared, to a universal reaction of outrage and scorn, Strawberry claimed he was misquoted. Somehow "the Franchise" neglected to include, as possible contributing factors to the team's failure, his own well-documented tendency to oversleep (in hotels and in right field), his public pouting matches with manager Davey Johnson, his swing at teammate and close friend Keith Hernandez, and his threat to beat up "that little redneck," Wally Backman, for daring to question his, Strawberry's, obvious periodic lack of desire. The little redneck, incidentally, was born and brought up in Oregon, and had never heard of the term "redneck" before.

(6) While not in Jerry Coleman's class, Kiner can get off some beauties. However, let me take this opportunity to point out that of all the broadcast talkers I have ever heard, in my opinion, he is the man I most enjoy listening to. His encyclopedic knowledge of the game, from the ins and

outs of everyday play, to baseball history and legend, to fascinating or amusing first-person anecdotes, is un-matched. Add to that his dignity, his decency, his gentle-manly good nature, and simple *joie de vivre,* and you've got one hell of a package. The next time I hear some jerk feeding his own ego on a radio sports call-in show by in-sulting Kiner and calling for his ouster from the Mets' broadcast booth, I will personally take a three-wood out to his neighborhood and practice my swing on his thick skull.

(7) The fact that he had been benched for nonproductivity may have had a little to do with Foster's complaint. To no-body's surprise, he also pleaded misquotation. To ice the cake, the player who replaced him in left field for the Mets was Mookie Wilson, the same race as Foster last time I looked.

(8) On being inducted into the Hall of Fame. The only way the story could have been improved on would be if the occasion had been for the Nobel Prize for Literature.

(9) In his notorious ghosted column in the New York *News,* which appeared the day he was to pitch the second game of the 1988 National League playoffs against the Dodgers. Lasorda's losers (the Mets had beaten them about ten times in a row) were so enraged, they bench-jockeyed the rookie out of his poise and into a defeat. This probably cost the Mets the pennant, since Cone had handled the Dodgers easily throughout his short career, and did so in the next game he pitched against them in the Series, after he'd re-covered from the L.A. team's shrewd psych-out.

Dominican Republic
All-Star Team*

First Base	**Cesar Cedeno**
Second Base	**Juan Samuel**
Shortstop	**Tony Fernandez**
Third Base	**Pedro Guerrero**
Outfield	**George Bell**
	Felipe Alou
	Manny Mota
Catcher	**Tony Pena**
Pitcher	**Juan Marichal**

Dominican Republic
All-Star Team
Notes

*Probably the most remarkable ethnic phenomenon in all of baseball is the disproportionate number of major league stars to emerge from the relatively tiny Dominican Republic. Their per capita numbers are staggering. In fact, we would not hesitate to match this Dominican team against any other all-star team in the collection. Wouldn't it be something to see the Sultan of Swat, who abhorred the change-up, trying to solve the befuddling collection of perfectly controlled breaking balls at the slow end of Marichal's extensive armory? And would Guerrero, who never met a fastball he couldn't devour, catch up to the hurry of the Johnsons, Fellers, Vances, Mungos?

Viva Santo Domingo!

45

Funny Name All-Star Team

First Base	**Mutz Ens**
Second Base	**Greg Legg**
Shortstop	**Coot Veal**
Third Base	**Fritz Von Kolnitz**
Outfield	**Everitt Booe**
	Tony Suck
	Spook Speake
Catcher	**Wes Blong**
Pitcher	**Ed Zmich**

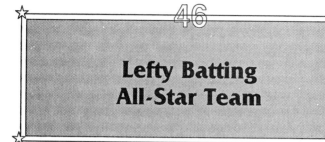

Lefty Batting
All-Star Team

First Base	**Lou Gehrig**
Second Base	**Eddie Collins**
Shortstop	**Arky Vaughan**
Third Base	**George Brett**
Outfield	**Babe Ruth**
	Ted Williams
	Ty Cobb
Catcher	**Yogi Berra**
Pitcher	**Lefty Grove**

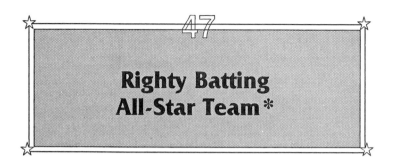

**Righty Batting
All-Star Team** *

First Base	**Foxx Greenberg**
Second Base	**Hornsby Lajoie**
Shortstop	**Wagner Boudreau**
Third Base	**Traynor Schmidt**
Outfield	**Clemente Mays**
	Aaron DiMaggio
	Heilmann Simmons
Catcher	**Campanella Bench**
Pitcher	**Dean Mathewson**

*(It's not always easy to make up your mind.)

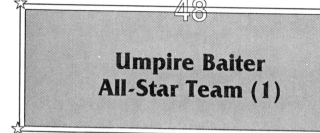

Umpire Baiter
All-Star Team (1)

First Base	**Frank Chance**
Second Base	**Billy Martin**
	Frank Frisch (2)
Shortstop	**Leo Durocher**
	Billy Jurges (3)
Third Base	**John McGraw (4)**
Outfield	**Babe Ruth (5)**
	Casey Stengel (6)
	Ty Cobb (7)
Catcher	**Ralph Houk (8)**
Pitcher	**Dallas Green (9)**

Umpire Baiter
All-Star Team
Notes

(1) The national style in sports is expressed most graphically in the attitude of the players toward the umpires, referees, linesmen who wield the power of victory or defeat over gangs (excuse me, I mean teams) of hard-muscled, aggressive young brutes. In Britain the very idea of questioning a cricket umpire's decision would be unthinkable, whereas in some third world countries, the fans' exhortations to kill the umpire are frequently taken literally. We fall somewhere in between.

To my knowledge, no umpire has ever been killed in organized baseball in the United States, although there are numerous cases on record of punches being thrown, one involving baseball's most prominent single individual. (See Note 5.)

(2) Most of our All-Star baiters developed their own trademarked *modus operandi* for tormenting their favorite arbiters. For Billy Martin, it was kicking dirt on them while testing how close he could fling his body in an umpire's direction without bumping him. An indication of how far baseball has progressed toward civilized behavior is that even Billy hasn't ever swung at an ump. A generation or two back, he would have joined the rough-and-tumble types in treating the boys in blue like marshmallow salesmen. Frank Frisch, the other half of the second-base ump-baiting entry, favored the screaming approach. I am sure the Jesuit fa-

thers at the Fordham Flash's alma mater in the Bronx would not have approved of his notorious lack of self-control. It was appropriate that Frisch's most fruitful years as a manager were spent leading charges by his St. Louis Cardinals, seemingly a whole team of ump baiters, boasting such goading specialists as Dizzy Dean, Ducky Medwick, Pepper Martin, and Lon Warneke. (The latter, ironically, having turned umpire himself after his arm lost its magic, was possibly the arbiter least tolerant of excessive protestation during his tenure.) Frisch, by the way, holds the record for blood vessels in the neck threatening to burst after a questionable call.

(3) The infield seems to have been a most fertile field for ump torturers, which is why we felt it necessary to name two second basemen, Martin and Frisch, and why there are two shortstops on the team. Durocher had a big mouth and was called Lippy during his playing days. As befits the show-biz type he became—marrying movie star Laraine Day and traveling with the Hollywood crowd—Leo early on incorporated the television cameras into his personal ump-baiting style. He would argue with the umpire to the accompaniment of broad arm gestures and well-thought-out body language, painstakingly pantomiming the points he was making for the benefit of the growing video audience. (This drove some umpires more nuts than his previous red-faced rages and bumpings.) Durocher and Jocko Conlan, a future Hall of Famer and one of the larger-muscled umpires in the history of this exacting occupation, were charter members of a mutual nonadmiration society. Once, in attempting to kick dirt on Conlan, Durocher missed the dirt (after all, he *was* known as the Hitless Wonder) and kicked the umpire's shins. Conlan immediately retaliated with his own kick to Leo's shins, thereby launching baseball's only shin fight between a player and an umpire. In another display of mutual affection and emotional maturity, in the course of a typical rabble-rousing Durocher protest, Conlan invited Durocher to take a punch at him. "Why?" asked the startled Lippy. "So I can knock your fucking block off," Conlan explained.

Billy Jurges, slick-fielding shortstop for the Cubs and

Giants of the thirties, had a relationship with National League umpire George Magerkurth comparable to Durocher's with Conlan. Once Jurges punched Magerkurth. Another time, during a heated argument, some of Billy's chaw juice "accidentally" sprayed the umpire's face. Magerkurth promptly returned a gob of his own spittle onto the temperamental shortstop's physiognomy. The spittin' contest continued until both participants realized how much amusement they were providing for everybody else in the ballpark and ceased the childish display.

(4) Ah, yes. McGraw. The original Baltimore Oriole, one of those who helped establish that team's reputation for ruthlessness and toughness. As a player, McGraw routinely attacked umpires physically. His approach was not much more genteel when he became a manager in the early 1900s. Among his exploits: He punched Bill Byron, the famous "Singing Umpire," noted for making controversial calls in rhyme and to music; hit Bob Emslie with a thrown ball; barred umpire Jimmy Johnstone from the ballpark; and even in his final years of managing the Giants, when an umpire drew his watch from his pocket to time McGraw's tirade, the Little Napoleon knocked it out of his hand and stomped it to smithereens.

Not even the immortal Bill Klem was safe from McGraw's rancor. His typical reaction to a rare bad call by Klem might be to clasp his hand to his head and fall backward in a simulated dead faint. Or it might be to scream imprecations worthy of an overly zealous marine drill sergeant. (He might get away with it if Klem—who was as just as he was fierce—agreed in his own mind that he'd blown the call. Otherwise it was not prudent to mess with Klem. Huge and utterly unrattleable, Klem could be swift and deadly in his retribution. He once cleared a bench because he decided they were jockeying a rookie pitcher too cruelly. And he invented the now common umpires' gambit of establishing their authority over a rookie by hitting him with obvious bad calls in his first big league at bats. (This is usually enough to knock any notion of defiance out of even the cockiest rook in short order.) Was even the monumental

Klem impervious to Muggsy's outrageous brand of perse-
cution? Klem, after decades of near-violent confrontation
with McGraw, would seem to have answered that question
neatly: "Whoever said sticks and stones may break my bones
but names can never hurt me never heard John McGraw."

(5) Babe Ruth was as tough on umpires as on pitchers. He
was suspended many times for "abusive language" to umpires, and he is at the center of one of the most bizarre
incidents in umpire-baiting history. Still in his pitching days,
the Babe objected strenuously to the home plate umpire's
call of the very first at bat—a base on balls. How strenuously? He attacked the ump with his fists. Even in that era
of open season on umpires, the Babe was ejected, and
fellow Red Sox pitcher Ernie Shore came on in relief. Shore
went on to pitch a perfect game and turn Ruth into an
asterisk, the first of two—the other, of course, being his
footnote to Roger Maris's home run record.

(6) Casey's ump-baiting career began in his minor league
days. In his delightful biography of Stengel, *You Could Look
It Up,* Maury Allen reports an incident witnessed by Dodgers scout Larry Sutton, who caught the feisty bush leaguer
playing for the Class C team of Aurora, Illinois. According
to Sutton's scouting report, when the umpire called Casey
out on a questionable third strike, then made another mistake by turning his back on him and bending over to whisk
off home plate, Stengel unhesitatingly whacked him across
his protruding rear with his bat. But even this brand of violence was not Stengel's normal style. His more usual
weapon was humor. As when a pitch in the dirt would be
called a strike, and he would get down in the batter's box
and swing from his knees, leading to the speculation that
Stengel's notorious ump baiting may have stemmed less
from any hostile intent than from his twin compulsions to
talk and to clown continuously. If not the ump or the opponents, then he would jockey his own teammates and
even talk to himself, usually in the process breaking up
everybody in the ballpark, which, in my opinion, was his
objective in the first place.

(7) The worst that can be said about Cobb's relations with umpires is that he handled them the same way he treated opposition players, annoying fans, and some of his own teammates—brutally, with violent hatred and physical assaults. The most famous of his many attacks on the men in blue was a rough-and-tumble he had with umpire Billy Evans, himself no cream puff. According to the legend, Cobb and Evans went at it for over an hour, pretty evenly matched, with nobody wanting to break up the fight and stop the two detested figures from continuing to damage one another.

(8) Having the most to lose from poor rapport with umpires, catchers are more inclined to be conciliatory than other position players. The constant dialogue among the crucial trio—batter, catcher, umpire—while frequently angry, generally tries to avoid the appearance of conflict, of "showing up" the ump. Most catchers are careful to face away from the ump in voicing their disagreement with a questionable call—the affable Gary Carter is an expert practitioner of this technique—to prevent the crowd from getting on him. Houk was the most emotional protester among the catchers I have seen. An ex-marine, capable of serious damage if unleashed, he is the only catcher I can recall having to be physically restrained during a "bad call seizure."

(9) Green should have been an infielder. He has the shortest fuse and the most physical approach to ump baiting of any pitcher—or former pitcher—I have been privileged to observe. I never saw Grimes, a known violent type, in any of his many disputes with the arbiters, and Dean, whom I did see, was similar to Stengel in being mostly talk and wisecracks. Lasorda talks a good fight, but the closest he comes to violence is his approach to a bowl of pasta. (Of course, having been a left-hander disqualifies him from any claim to consistency whatsoever, so I take back any predictions I may have made. On second thought, I won't be surprised if Lasorda attacks Ron Luciano with a carving knife.) The loveliest case of umpire baiting I know involves Dummy

Taylor, a deaf pitcher who won 117 games for the Giants in the early part of the century. Dummy, no dummy he, was a proficient ump baiter despite his handicap. His sign-language ridicule and pantomined complaints were maddeningly frustrating to umpires who couldn't find any grounds on which to retaliate. It was simply impossible for them to prove that what he was signing merited any penalty. My favorite of Dummy's gags was his Harpoesque unspoken comment on an umpire's decision not to call a game during a heavy downpour. Taylor returned to the mound wearing a pair of fisherman's hipboots. I also like the apocryphal tale of Dummy's only comeuppance at the hands of an ump. Seems an arbiter came into the league who had a deaf relative and was familiar with deaf signing. He gleefully nailed the startled Taylor, and tossed him out of the game—in sign language.

A.K.A. (Also Known As) All-Star Team

First Base	**Harold Arthur Troyavesky (1)**
Second Base	**Casimir Eugen Kwietniewski (2)**
Shortstop	**John Michael Paveskovich (3)**
Third Base	**Francesco Stephano Pezzolo (4)**
Outfield	**Antonio Machado (5)**
	Aloys Szymanski (6)
	Maximilian Carnarius (7)
Catcher	**Cornelius Alexander McGillicuddy (8)**
Pitcher	**Fernand Anguamea Anguamea (9)**

(For their baseball names, turn the page!)

Their Baseball I.D.s

(1) Hal Trosky

(2) Cass Michaels

(3) Johnny Pesky

(4) Ping Bodie

(5) Tony Armas

(6) Al Simmons

(7) Max Carey

(8) Connie Mack

(9) Fernando Valenzuela

50

Base Stealer (Season) All-Star Team*

First Base	**Frank Chance**	67	(1903)
Second Base	**Eddie Collins**	81	(1910)
Shortstop	**Maury Wills**	104	(1962)
Third Base	**Buck Herzog**	48	(1911)
Outfield	**Rickey Henderson**	130	(1982)
	Lou Brock	118	(1974)
	Vince Coleman	110	(1985)
Catcher	**John Wathan**	36	(1982)
Pitcher	**Nixey Callahan**	45	(1911)

Base Stealer
All-Star Team
Notes

*Stealing bases was allegedly not Buck Herzog's only lar-
cenous endeavor. The Cubs' then second baseman was
called to testify in Chicago during the Black Sox trial, after
a witness accused him of conspiring with Hal Chase, the
Giants' brilliant but larcenous first baseman, to fix a game
between the teams. Herzog denied the allegation and got
away with it, although his career did end that year. Nixey
Callahan was the poor man's Babe Ruth. Like the Babe, he
won more than ninety games in the big leagues as a pitcher
before becoming a regular outfielder with the White Sox.
There the resemblance ends with a crash. A .273 singles
hitter over his thirteen years as an active player, Callahan
had mysterious lapses in midcareer: He was out of the majors from 1906 through 1910, returning in 1911 for three
additional years. Whatever, the remarkable explosion in recent years in what was thought to be a lost art, starting
with Maury Wills and continuing through Lou Brock and
Rickey Henderson and now the seemingly unstoppable
Vince Coleman, is in my opinion the single greatest ad-
vance the game has seen.

51

Non-Hall of Fame
All-Star Team

First Base	**Gil Hodges**
Second Base	**Joe Gordon (1)**
Shortstop	**Phil Rizzuto (2)**
Third Base	**Ken Boyer**
Outfield	**Joe Jackson**
	Pete Reiser (3)
	Reggie Smith (4)
Catcher	**Wally Schang (5)**
Pitcher	**Wes Ferrell (6)**

Non-Hall of Fame
All-Star Team
Notes

(1) Now that Red Schoendienst has finally gotten his due, what's holding up Tony Lazzeri's induction into the Hall? And if Bobby Doerr is in, what—or who—is barring the door to Joe Gordon, who vied with Doerr as the class of major league second sackers during the late thirties and forties? In the opinion of this witness, who saw them both, Doerr couldn't carry Gordon's glove, much less match his home run power. Let's be fair!

(2) Speaking of being fair. Holy cow, Old-Timers Committee guys, give the Scooter Man a break, for cry eye!

(3) By naming Reiser—and some others—to the NON-HALL OF FAME All-Star Team, we do not necessarily claim niches for them in the Hall. It's just that there is a gang of marvelous players who for one reason or another do not qualify. Reiser, for an obvious example, battered himself out of contention by running into enough walls to end his career long before achieving the unwritten required minimum longevity. Shoeless Joe, for that infamous reason, is automatically disqualified.

(4) Smith is one of a sizable group of outfielders I admire inordinately for their honest, dedicated, day-in day-out consistently high level of performance. Al Oliver, Dusty Baker,

Garry Maddox, Gary Matthews, Hal McRae may not have rung up numbers worthy of elevation to the Hall, but they are all quality players I would want on my team when the chips are down.

(5) With numbers almost identical to those of his nearly exact contemporary Ray Schalk, Schang is Rizzuto to Schalk's Reese. Neither has been permitted to join his opposite number in the Hall of Fame. Since both Schang and Rizzuto were Yankees, it could be inferred that some anti-New York prejudice is at work here. If so, knock it off, boys. New York is part of America, like it or not.

(6) Several other candidates present themselves. Carl Mays (his chances no doubt damaged by his distinction as the killer, by beaning, of Ray Chapman, of the only major league ballplayer ever slain in action), Eddie Cicottte (doomed to exile from the Hall for the same reason as Black Sox teammate Joe Jackson), Urban Shocker, Ed Reulbach—all multiple-20 game winners. We like Ferrell because his pitching numbers are as good as anybody's and he was a hell of a hitter. Besides, if he were inducted, the Hall would have its first brother battery, with Rick Ferrell now having made it (ironically, Wes probably deserves it more than Rick). It would be no contest were Ferguson Jenkins not a convicted drug abuser. His stats are unquestionably Hall-of-Fame caliber.

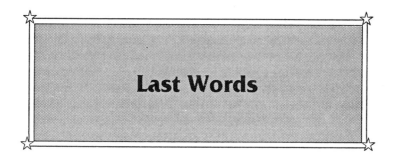

Last Words

Thank you, Say Hey Willie, Joltin' Joe, Shoeless Joe, Smokey Joe, Jumpin' Joe, Bambino, Big Poison, Little Poison, Larrupin' Lou, Sweet Lou, Stan the Man, Spaceman, Lippy, Dizzy, Daffy, Dazzy, Goofy, Old Reliable, Mr. October, Big Six, Penguin, Scrap Iron, Rajah, Honus, Yogi, Mickey, Campy, Pee Wee, Charlie Hustle, Yaz, Maz, Thumper, Ozark Ike, Daddy Wags, Memphis Bill, Country, Wizard of Oz, Gorgeous George, Bucketfoot Al, Scooter, Shotgun, Spoke, Hammerin' Hank, Old Aches and Pains, Highpockets, Schnozz, Harvard Eddie, Laughing Larry, Dirty Jack, Cha-Cha, Stretch—and all you others.

We couldna done it withoutcha!

Did we leave out your favorite team? Do you disagree with any of our choices? Send us your own All-Star Team! (Mail to: Al Davis and Elliot Horne, c/o William Morrow and Company, 105 Madison Avenue, New York, N.Y. 10016.)

The _____
All-Star Team

First Base   _____

Second Base   _____

Shortstop   _____

Third Base   _____

Outfield   _____

                        _____

                        _____

Catcher   _____

Pitcher   _____